"*Live Your Vacation* is a timely message for the world. Gloria reminds us to take our journey inward to the joys of our highest and best self, and live our dream life today and every day by engaging with and seeing others at this level. She has included many practical applications of spiritual wisdom – read several times and complete the exercises that resonate for you."

— DR LANCE SECRETAN, Bestselling author of *The Spark, The Flame and The Torch,* business consultant and advisor to leaders

"Gloria's book is simple yet powerful. Though it is a result of her journey and those of her clients, you will recognize spiritual wisdom to apply to your life."

— AZIM JAMAL, # 1 Amazon bestselling co-author of *The Power of Giving*

"Gloria's book comes from her deep rooted commitment to making a difference in the lives of others. She creates an easy to follow pathway for anyone interested in exploring the possibility of doing things differently in their lives. I especially like the section on 'shedding your baggage,' because that 'baggage' is often what holds us back from being able to create a rich and fulfilling life for ourselves, our family and friends. Gloria's gentle compassion is the thread that holds this all together. Read and discover how you too can create a journey within."

— JIM STANTON, Communications Consultant of **jim-stanton.com**

"Gloria's profound book, *Live Your Vacation,* is a 'reflection' of how fully Gloria lives her life and how deeply she touches and inspires others to live their lives with purpose, passion, and meaning! Gloria lives what she writes, and this is why her words have such a powerful impact and inspires the reader to take 'action'!"

— BROCK TULLY, Author of *Reflections* books, Co-Founder of the *Kindness Foundation of Canada*, Cyclist for kindness at **brocktully.com**

"I have had the pleasure and privilege of being coached by Gloria for over 4 years and she has inspired me to believe in myself and feel confident that my life is full and abundant and as she is always saying: *"You are magnificent just as you are"*. Her book expresses fully her values and what she has coached me on to live my vacation. She has helped me most to express myself with love. Her favourite quote to me is *"speak your truth lovingly without fear of the outcome"*. I have done that and live my life now with compassion for myself and others. Thank you Gloria!"

— Lilly Page, Image Consultant,
Founder of **flairimage.ca**

"I have always wanted to live my "Dream Life" today but was always too busy to do so and never took the time to figure out how to escape from my current paradigm. Part of the problem was that I needed a "Road Map" to find my way. Little did I know that help was on the way. In *Live Your Vacation,* Gloria Tom Wing Staudt has developed a handbook for success, and by following this template, I truly believe that I now may be able to leave my old life behind and begin living my dream life today.

I have known Gloria for a number of years. She is a friend, a mentor, and a pathfinder. Her formal education in Psychology, coupled with the insights gained from her professional life, have given her a very credible perspective of what works and what doesn't work. Gloria has seen the damage caused by the workaholic syndrome and she has always preached the benefit of life balance. I trust her instincts. This book makes good sense."

— T.A. (Terry) Henfrey, Businessman

"Gloria is a gifted intuitive coach who uncovers with compassion and enthusiasm a direct path to your soul's joy. Her book is a treasure of clarity. It is a 'workbook' in the best sense. Much like Napoleon Hill's *Think and Grow Rich.*

You will want to return to Gloria's book again and again for inspiration, instruction and guidance. She shows you a step-by-step process for clearing away the chaos and reconnecting with your soul's true desires.

As a firm believer that life is a boring vacuum without a defined purpose and juicy, soul-fulfilling goals, Gloria will help you see who you are, define your Life's Vision, shed the baggage, walk you through the 7 core principles for living a life on purpose, stay conscious and awake at the wheel, celebrate your wins and come full circle, home to yourself. Gloria will help you find the What to your Why and back again! I intend to use this book as a resource for my own self-development and will continue to recommend it to my clients."

— BAETH DAVIS, The Hand Analyst Founder
at **handanalyst.com**

"There is much to life but unless we take the little steps and follow the right sequence with the right attitudes and habits, we will miss on what matters most.

Gloria Tom Wing Staudt's first book: *Live your Vacation – The Ultimate Guide to Live Your Dream Life... Every Day!* is a book to be read for self-development and for leading and inspiring others to get the most of life... and to be reread many more times... It is clear, practical, and written in a very appealing tone."

— MARIO R GATUS, President, Rotary Club
Makati Central (1997-98),
R. I. District 3830 Philippines

"Throughout both the professional and personal sides of my life, particularly during my 33 years in the Canadian Forces, I continually sought to define myself and my role in this world. It was only during the latter stages of my military career when I was Commandant of the Royal Military College of Canada, and upon retirement when I spent considerable time understanding from a spiritual sense why God had placed me in on this earth, that I started to become "comfortable in my skin". But what a difficult, complex, and frustrating journey it was getting to this stage of self-realization.

With her book, *Live Your Vacation,* Gloria Tom Wing Staudt lays out the signposts for your own personal life journey, thus reducing the "trial and error" road I experienced. Armed with the insights she provides, you can better prepare yourself for the challenges, bumps and detours we encounter in everyday living by having a vision for the various aspects of your life, by shedding the baggage that impedes your progress, and by adopting a simple set of spiritual principles to use on a daily basis when confronted with the realities of life.

John Lennon once said, "Life is what happens when you are busy making plans". I certainly agree with him, but I would counter that "Wise people make life plans, but understand they will need constant refinement."

— Brigadier-General (retired) Ken Hague

"The table of contents page in Gloria's book *Live your Vacation* reveals clear signposts guiding you onto a path that can take you to a land many dream of but where few actually reside... the place of living your life with the feeling of being on permanent vacation. Follow these signposts into the wisdom in this book and begin a very personal and rewarding journey to your new home."

— Reg Neufeld,
Founder of **GrowingIntoSuccess.com**

"Through our work together my view of my life was transformed and she has taught me how to deal with my fears. The vibrant faith which she lives by daily, her unconditional love and understanding for all people everywhere is a tremendous example to me and inspires me to think, *"what would Gloria do?"* Her book reflects the practical and spiritual approach of our work together. I am grateful to her for my transformations."

— Mary Anne Barcelona Collins,
Opera Singer, **Maryannebarcellona.com**

"I have worked with Gloria during the transition from a job I did not really enjoy in an unsupportive workplace to becoming self-employed by using my skills and creative gifts. It was terrifying and when I look back over the past few years, I don't know how I could have gotten here without Gloria's quiet, honouring support. She is amazing with her integrity, strength and insight. She has assisted me to find a clear sense of who I am. What a gift to be able to do that for others. You begin to experience her work through this book so you too can start on your journey to live your vacation."

— Daine Halley, Interior Designer, Project Manager, Founder of **cometinteriordesign.com**

"Gloria speaks and writes from her inner being. In Live Your Vacation, she provides an insight to, and addresses life's journey."

— Horace C. Armoogum, Speaker and Business Consultant

"I am grateful to Gloria Tom Wing Staudt for sharing her philosophy and teachings that honour you wherever you are in your life and career. This book is a garden of hope filled with gentle reminders of the abundance that awaits you every day and the steps you can take right now to start getting what you want and deserve in the sacred path of your life. This is one book I will treasure and return to time and time again for renewal and daily inspiration."

— Richard Van Camp, Bestselling author of *The Lesser Blessed* and internationally renowned storyteller

GLORIA TOM WING STAUDT

Live *your* Vacation

The Ultimate Guide to Living Your Dream Life... Every Day!

Love Your Life

Live Your Vacation: The Ultimate Guide to Living Your Vacation... Every Day!

Published by:
Love Your Life Publishing
PO Box 2, Dallastown, PA 17313
www.LoveYourLifeBooks.com

ISBN: 978-0-9820477-5-0
Library of Congress Control No.: 2010927143

Cover design, layout and typesetting by Cyanotype Book Architects
Editors: Charlon Bobo, EditCopyProof
Tara Schiro, Write with Grace
Author Photo by Michael Ford, Vancouver, BC, Canada

Printed in the United States of America
♲ Printed on recycled paper

A portion of the proceeds from the sale of this book will be donated to The Rotary Foundation of Rotary International to help fund Peace Fellowships through the Rotary Centers for International Studies in Peace and Conflict Resolution Program.

DEDICATION

To my mom, Kam Chee and my late dad James,
for the gift of unconditional love and faith

QUOTATION

Remember Who You Are... a Masterpiece

You were born a Masterpiece
with a song in your heart and music in your soul
ready to be expressed in your unique way
You are on a divine journey
with a special contribution to make by serving one another
You are called to be your highest and best self
with the courage and wisdom to be true to yourself and others
You deserve to live a life of your dreams
with love and generosity to leave your legacy for generations to come
You are meant to shine brilliantly
with ease and joy, trusting the wisdom of your intuition
You are a Masterpiece
with love in your heart, do your best and let go of the rest
You are connected, in love, to other Masterpieces
Remember the Masterpiece you are

— Gloria Tom Wing Staudt

TABLE OF CONTENTS

ACKNOWLEDGEMENTS

"Gratitude is the fairest blossom which springs from the soul."
— HOWARD WARD BEECHER

IT IS WITH DEEP APPRECIATION THAT I EXPRESS MY gratitude to all who have crossed my path leading to the writing of this, my first book. It has been a memorable journey, rich in many ways. I was inspired by my own evolution and the desire to inspire others to honor their deepest yearnings and share their gifts.

To God, my greatest source of inspiration and guidance. I am grateful to you for orchestrating all the many blessings you have given me, to see and appreciate my role as your instrument, to inspire others, and be inspired by them, to live the masterpiece we were born to manifest. Writing this book is one example of a blessing for which I am grateful. My life reflects my eternal gratitude.

To all my clients, customers, mentors, hundreds of Peak Success Inspiration quotation newsletter subscribers, Burnaby Metrotown Rotary club members and other Rotary District 5040 Rotarians who have given me the honor and privilege to serve and be inspired by you, and in so doing, revealed to me the joy in giving and receiving. Thank you from my heart to yours.

To Luis Aguilar who first encouraged me to write for a newspaper and then to write a book, and for his family's love, support and prayers. You shared your message of a call for me to write and share in a bigger way. I extend my eternal gratitude to you and your family, especially for Abue's loving prayers.

To my clients who directly inspired this book, affirming the results of your deep commitment to your highest and best selves and connecting to your highest source of power, truth and grace. Daine, thank you for the gift of the title of this book as it was expressed in one of our coaching conversations. Thank you to Lilly, Mary Anne, Annie, Kenneth, Barb, Gaynor and Barnuka for beta testing various aspects of this book and for being a source of inspiration.

To James Roche, the Info Product Guy, thank you for helping me to clearly see the magic of my core gifts as a process to be shared. I appreciate and I am inspired by your core gifts and authenticity.

To Christine Kloser, publisher with a heart of gold, thank you for your ever generous love in helping me manifest the author in me. You are an inspiration; I appreciate all your loving guidance.

To Richard Van Camp, best selling author and internationally renowned story teller, my eternal gratitude for the generous heartfelt care you have shown in guiding me as I learned to show up in my writing as I show up in person.

To my mother, Kam Chee, each of my loving brothers & sisters, many family members, very dear lifelong friends near and far, and my coach Jean Pierre, your unconditional love and support touch me deeply and make it possible for me to do what I do every day. I am forever grateful.

To my husband Richard and daughter Alison, you are my everyday inspiration to be my highest and best self, to love and be loved. I am thankful for all I have learned through the gift of your love and presence in my life.

PREFACE

THANK YOU FOR BEING CURIOUS ABOUT THIS BOOK and for choosing to read it. My desire in writing this book is to share my message to readers worldwide, inspiring each of you to live in a state of love, to connect with all that makes you happy and to share that with others. In the "Discover Who You Are" section of Chapter 1, I share my personal discovery to inspire you to take your inward journey for your own discovery. Your awareness to take action begins there.

The core of my message is particularly relevant today because more than ever we need to consciously get back to the basics of seeing the truth of who we really are, align with our highest source and be loving and kind in our thoughts, words and actions. In doing so, we relearn to trust ourselves and others and to creatively collaborate with each other for the greater good of all.

You will see a reference to God, and it is there as my personal reference and not as a reference to any particular religion for you. You may have a different reference that works for you for that universal source of higher loving energy referred to as Buddha, Creator, Universe, Hashem, Allah, Spirit, Almighty etc., all of which is respected and honored.

Reading this book is not an accident; keep it as a close friend to remind you of the masterpiece you are and to honor your desire to be happy every day; to live your dream life every day. It is your easy reference and no matter what stage you are in (reminding yourself of who you are, what excess baggage you need to shed, what essentials are useful in the moment, what principles will support you, what you are to celebrate, what daily habits you are to honor, the reminder that you have the answers within), just the right message will be there for you. For you and your loved ones I wish you blissful happiness and for this book to be the catalyst to all transformations resulting from the actions you take every day.

Celebrate every day of your life for it is your divine journey.

With Love, hugs and blessings in abundance,

Gloria

INTRODUCTION

LIVE YOUR VACATION. PEOPLE'S RESPONSES TO THIS title have been positive… I want that. I need that. Yes, I live for my vacations. I am on vacation. My life is a vacation. My friend Horace said, "Life is a Vacation. Success is living your dreams."

How does being on your ideal vacation feel?

Happy. Excited. Relaxed. Energized. Healthy. Stress-free. Carefree. Full of freedom, fun and enjoyment.

In your dream life, every day feels like a vacation day. You enjoy each day. You live each day fully alive, fully awake, and fully conscious about what you think, say and do. You are authentic to who you are; your heart, mind, and soul are aligned and you show up powerfully each day as you are, true to yourself and to others. You enjoy good health and handle everything with ease, regardless of circumstances. When you remember the times you feel inner calm and trust in yourself and something greater than you, what happens externally will not disturb your power within.

"No storm can shake my inmost calm…"

—WORDS FROM A PRAYER SONG
"HOW CAN I KEEP FROM SINGING"
Trust page 616, *Glory & Praise 2nd Edition*

Need versus Want

Needing a vacation likely means you are living and working under much stress and want to escape your current experience. The stress is overwhelming and at various levels you are not experiencing joy. You are taking greater care of others than you are of yourself.

Wanting and choosing to go away on a vacation is not the same as needing a vacation.

This book is about living what seems ordinary in life in an extra ordinary way. It is about me and yet also about you. It is about being awake to the masterpiece you were born as and fully expressing who you are on a daily basis. It is about being fully conscious and present in your life knowing that your life matters. You will have read or heard similar messages from others who have inspired you to take positive action. This book is about bringing love into your day every day without NEEDING to go on vacation to feel the impact of love. Throughout the ages, the core messages have been the same regardless of nationality, culture, religion or ethnic heritage. The core timeless messages all relate to LOVE which elevates you and others directly and indirectly through you. When you live each day BEING loving in who you are and what you do, you will be living your vacation.

You might be wondering Who is Gloria? and why would I listen to what she has to say about how to live my vacation?

The contents of this book are the result of my own learning experiences as well as those of my clients. I trust you will find something of value for you.

The guideline I follow is simple and requires practice.

BE LOVING. More specifically,

- come from a loving place in all interactions,
- see others through loving eyes and an open heart,
- be of service.

- bring joy into your day every day. This means on a daily basis doing things that bring you joy and finding the joy in whatever you are committed to doing.

My life is a constant balance of family and friends, business and community with spiritual connection as the basis of it all. What gives me joy as I live my vacation includes and is not limited to the following:

Spiritual Connection

When I am spiritually connected, I am energized, feel rejuvenated and easily accomplish whatever I set out to do.

My Joy comes from:

- Spending quiet time to pray and be grateful
- Relaxing for a minimum 30minute aromatherapy bath
- Reading at church knowing that my voice touches at the soul level
- Enjoying nature leisurely kayaking in British Columbia's Burrard Inlet or New York's Schroon Lake
- Walking near any lake, beach or ocean
- Listening to a variety of music including James Twyman's 12 prayers.

Family and Friends

Through the highs and lows of being married to Richard, it gives me great joy to know that I had fallen in love again after 20 years of marriage.

As I write this, another source of great joy, gratitude and inspiration is the thought that Alison, our 17 year old daughter is still comfortable to hug and kiss me in public, will speak to me about what is occurring in her life and often speak words of wisdom that even surprise her as soon as she expresses a truth.

My heart is very full to know how blessed we are to live together with Mama who loves us unconditionally. She always thinks of us and each of her children and grandchildren, ready to help cook and serve in the most loving way.

Another source of my joy and good fortune is in each family member and friends here in Canada and United States who are always ready to help whenever I ask.

Some of my joy filled activities include:

- Savoring food with family and friends
- Lovingly making a meal or baking cookies to give away
- Following my intuition in determining gifts to give away and beautifully wrapping them
- Leisurely kayaking or hiking with Richard, Alison, and brother in law Bob
- Connecting deeply at soul level while having meaningful conversations
- Being helpful to my family and friends and sharing their joys
- Celebrating Christmas and all holidays with family and friends.

Business

I feel energized, inspired and it gives me great joy:

- Observing and celebrating client's transformation and their variety of successes as defined by them
- Witnessing their lives, relationships and businesses enhanced
- Listening for what gives others joy and seeing clearly their brilliance
- Having the deep meaningful conversations that empowers them to take greater care of themselves, honor the person they are and the highest desires of their heart and soul
- Celebrating their breakthroughs and dreams come true

- Guiding teams to be high functioning, honoring their brilliance
- Facilitating authentic conversations
- Collaborating and strategizing to create wins for everyone involved.

Community

I feel a sense of satisfaction sharing my leadership talents in the service of my community locally and globally through Rotary, church, and Burnaby Board of Trade

- Making a positive difference for the highest good of all and our environment
- Honoring and enjoying the talents of other volunteers
- Celebrating everyone's wins and a sense of community.

As a wife, mother, daughter, family member, friend, conscious entrepreneur, personal success coach, member of Rotary and person of the world, my deep joys also come from:

- Feeling healthy and knowing that my family is also healthy
- Expressing my appreciation for those in my life and business
- Planting or arranging flowers for joy and beauty
- Seeing beauty in people, things and nature
- Feel happy and seeing others happy
- Finding inspiration in all challenges
- Sharing positive energy with others
- Listening powerfully for who people are and enjoying their essence
- Noticing the similarities that connect us all and the differences that enrich us all
- Seeing God's divine presence in daily occurrences

For those of you who are curious about what shaped what I have to say and why you might consider any of it…

What I have to offer is also a result of my:

- **education and training** (Masters degree in Psychology, certification in behavioral and values assessments, coach training)
- **work experiences** (teacher, bank teller, university alumni activities organizer, corporate project co-ordinator, personal success coach, life strategist, workshop facilitator)
- **life experiences** (mother, wife, daughter, sister, family member, friend)
- **volunteer leadership experiences** (Rotary Club of Burnaby Metrotown President & various director and chair roles, Burnaby Board of Trade Business Excellence Awards Chair, St. Helen's School Graduation Committee Chair).

The strategies and approaches I developed and practiced were inspired and influenced by many mentors and coaches, my own divine journey and those with whom I crossed paths along the way. A significant conscious beginning was during my teenage years reading Norman Vincent Peale's "The Power of Positive Thinking." Surrendering to God's will where I am part of a larger cohesive plan, was a lesson I learned over the years. This lesson and wisdom from various teachers led to my belief that everything happens for our highest good with blessings that come in the form of difficult and challenging disguises.

Needless to say not everything in my life ended up the way I originally had in mind but upon reflection, I see the blessings.

Here is an example: Celebrating my graduation with a Bachelor's degree in Psychology was special because I was happy for my parents who had no formal education and worked hard so their children would be educated. I applied for a Clinical Psychology Doctoral Program and was rejected because I was too much of a "Pollyanna" in my interview responses. That confused me and I questioned who I was. It was not until years later during a coach training class that

I saw the truth about myself and my gift, as being optimistic in my outlook and my approach to life and people. That insight guided me to confidently keep seeing the greater and positive truth of who people are, and the magnificent masterpiece they were born to be, even when they do not see it themselves.

I am an expert on Inner Peace. Not the kind where I lived in solitude broke open and became whole, but the kind involving an awakening to who I am *in the midst* of my human challenges. It allowed me to recognize my worth, transform my relationships to find inner peace and calm, recognize my divine journey through life, and trust my highest source of power, joys and inspirations. All of this is reflected in my dedication to give of my best every day in guiding and facilitating those committed to their own awakening.

I am fully present to my clients listening powerfully, intuitively and without judgment on who they are, where they are in the moment, what blocks the pathway and what their soul's desires are waiting to express with courage and love. Your journey to inner peace is a personal one. The most life transforming decision you can make is to go on an inward journey to live and enjoy your life, fully awake and fully conscious, to be present to yourself and to others on a daily basis. Yes, it is possible. I did it and so can YOU.

The development of this book began in my childhood. I grew up in Trinidad when vacation was not a word I knew, but I knew the feeling. It showed up as a day when we took a drive on long winding roads to Mayaro beach, parked near coconut trees, played on the sand and in the warm, salty water and had a more-than-usual delicious homemade lunch from the trunk of Papa's car.

Those days of having nothing to do but play and have fun… hmm that feeling of excitement, the breeze in my hair, the smell of salty ocean water and the feel of the waves splashing on my feet and body and running back and forth to knee deep water; not a care in the world, feeling very happy.

> *"Success is not the key to happiness. Happiness is the key to success. If you love what you are doing, you will be successful."*
>
> — HERMAN CAIN, accomplished business person, speaker, writer

That feeling of happiness when experienced in every area of your life—using your talents and making a difference in the world as you choose—is your dream life. Why postpone that happiness of a dream life until you have this or that? Instead, have it now, be happy now, and have that ideal vacation feeling now. That's the essential message of this book.

Perhaps you, too, have a special memory of precious times with your family and friends; going to your favorite cabin or vacation home for one day, a weekend, or those much-anticipated two weeks away from home, or a business or work experience that thrilled you to your core. You felt fully alive; in a quiet unassuming way or an enthusiastic, emotionally expressive way. Whatever way you feel joy from the depths of your soul, you already know the feeling of living your vacation.

Even if the messages you read in this book are already what you have read, heard or know at some level intellectually, what matters most now is the inspired actions you resonate with and commit to taking after reading any part of this book.

To maximize the benefit of this book, I provide a journal as a bonus for purchasing this book. By going through the exercises, you will deepen your learning and better-implement the principles. Go to **www.liveyourvacation.com** to download it and use it immediately. Use it to support you in gaining clarity and taking action steps to be happy every day. Consider also sharing your progress or challenges with a friend to support each other in your precious journey.

My desire is for you to be your best, highest, and authentic self with peace, harmony, joy, and fulfillment every day. Yes, every day. I want you to be fully awake and present to your whole life, in which you see possibilities in the face of every challenge and then fully express the masterpiece you are.

Live Your Vacation!

With Love, hugs and blessings in abundance,

CHAPTER 1

Experience the Journey Within

Discover Who You Are

YOU WERE BORN A MASTERPIECE! YOU ARE MEANT to make a unique contribution in the world, simply by being your best and highest self, shining with brilliance. This is who you really are. However, you've probably noticed that in living this experience of bliss, it's not as easy as you'd like it to be.

Living your bliss, or as I like to say *Living Your Vacation*, is a journey. It's a journey of your heart, your mind, and your soul. It's this inner journey—and fully expressing the core of 'who you really are'—that makes every single day feel like a vacation day (no matter your unique circumstances).

To begin this journey of experiencing your dream life every day, you must start at the beginning by asking yourself the ultimate question of life, "Who am I?"

One thing I can tell you for sure is you are not your identification. Just think about anytime you are asked for I.D. You pull out your driver's license, identification card, or passport as if that was your identification. Not exactly.

So, let's start at the very beginning so you can embark on this journey of discovery, celebrate who you really are, and how you came to be who you are. There are three distinct steps to taking this journey of self-exploration:

1. Others See Who You Are
2. You See Who You Are

3. You See Who Others Are.

Let me explain.

Others See Who You Are

The first discovery or awareness of who you are usually comes from how others describe you. It can also come from your perception of what others think about you. I'm sure if you reflect back on your life and think of the family, neighbors, teachers, friends and colleagues who have crossed your path, you will remember how those people thought of and described you.

For example, as I reflect back on my own life, there are many people whom I recall describing me from their perspective. Here are a few of those memories:

Mei Fong, my aunt and second mom (who spoke no English), was the woman with whom I spent most of my early childhood. She taught me the ToiSand/Taishan dialect of the Chinese language. I remember overhearing her as she proudly shared with visitors how I kept my clothes closet neatly organized and how respectful and sincere-of-heart I was. As a young child, hearing my cherished aunt describe me as organized, respectful, and sincere was a significant piece of beginning to know myself.

My mom described how curious I was; always asking questions. Many times she felt she did not have the answers. Knowing that she encouraged my curiosities gave me the permission to be curious and to nurture that aspect of my nature.

My high school teachers saw leadership abilities before I did and appointed me captain of one school group, class leader, and later the "head girl" of the school. That last appointment was a surprise as I thought another, more talented, outgoing and popular student would have been chosen. They saw what I did not yet see in myself.

At university, my resident assistant peers voted me "Resident Assistant of the Year" upon graduation. That gave me a special feeling of who I was as a foreign student from a small island succeeding in a big New York university.

Throughout my life, what others saw was the way I learned about myself. It's likely you, too, have seen yourself through the eyes of others, and through the impact of your experiences. Take time to reflect on how others saw you in different stages of your life (Preschool, Elementary School, High School, College/University, your first job, your current business/work). Sit in an inspiring spot, in a comfortable place at home, at the local library, out in nature, at the beach, lake, garden, river, or anywhere you feel relaxed and carefree; you will be inspired. Allow your pen, pencil, computer keyboard or audio recorder to flow freely and capture your insights. Note any patterns emerging and how you feel about what they mean to you now.

JOURNAL ENTRY GUIDE #1

Assessing each stage of your life, record what you remember and how you felt.

You See Who You Are

"Being authentic sometimes requires us to be humble, to reveal our foibles or imperfections."— Dr. Lance Secretan, bestselling author, business consultant and advisor to leaders

The next discovery in your self exploration is to embark on the inner journey to the core, or essence, of who you are. This step is about gently heightening your awareness and consciousness, listening to—and trusting—your intuition, and making conscious choices with your discovery.

Discovering who you are is a 3-stage process:

1. You were asleep
2. You awoke
3. You explore and discover.

Let's explore each of these points in greater depth.

1. You were asleep

For many reasons during this stage you were asleep to who you really are, you were unaware of the basis of all your decisions or choices, you weren't able to pay close attention to subtle nuances, you were in an unconscious state-of-being. There is no judgment as to the reason why that is so; it is simply your experience, which is a necessary part of your divine journey.

You may recognize yourself in the following scenarios:

- You went to school, got a job, and trained for a profession or career because you thought you should; maybe you have innate talent in a particular area or it was expected of you. Then you got married and had children, creating the image of a "normal" life
- You attended college and then went to work instead of post secondary school because family finances were not available or you simply wanted to make money. You wanted to be self-sustaining and you did well, but you've had many failed relationships. You yearn for one meaningful connection that is permanent. At the moment, every day is somewhat predictable
- You went to school, have a business or career in which you work

many long hours, but you are challenged by your personal relationships. You have difficulty justifying time spent on yourself and feel guilty for not making more time for family and friends.

Life happens, and over time, you may lose touch with who you really are. This is especially true if you have learned to:

- listen to the voice of others, over and above your own voice
- assume the role and responsibility of nurturer or caretaker, super-man or super-woman, or fix-it person.

You recognize you are "out of touch with yourself" when your state of happiness is dependent on how others behave, what they say, or other prominent clues that surface:

- you don't know or remember your deepest desires or what you truly enjoy
- you are afraid of being alone because you do not feel fully alive when alone. Alone is lonely and perhaps even scary
- you feel aches and pains in your body more often than not; you are not as healthy as you would like to be; you may be unhappy about your weight
- life feels like you are often on a roller coaster of highs and lows
- even though you have everything and you are grateful for it all, you feel life is monotonous.

Do you see your life in any of these scenarios? Are you asleep or not feeling fully alive? Do you feel something is missing but don't know exactly what it is?

A "Yes" answer acknowledges you are/were asleep.

2. You awoke

The catalyst for waking up in—and to—your life is different for each of us. It may arise from a deep pain of not feeling loved, from the inability to realize your worth, or from feeling that there must be something more but you are just not sure what it is.

My journey of discovery began with a spiritual awakening during one of the most vulnerable times of my life; when our daughter Alison was a baby. I felt overwhelmed and alone even though I was surrounded by loved ones. As an older, sleep-deprived new mom I was out of my familiar thriving environment as an independent career woman with a confident and fearless sense of endless possibilities for my future.

As I lay in bed in the early dark hours of the morning, I felt an uneasy, gripping fear of helplessness. I remember a distinct awakened moment and the commitment I made soon afterwards. The awakening was a feeling of great relief and lightness, when in faith I surrendered everything to God in prayer. (Dear God, please help me. The weight I feel is too heavy and I can no longer do this by myself. I am sorry for forgetting that you are always there and will not abandon me. Jesus, I trust in you to guide me. Give me the courage to change what I can change, the patience for what I cannot change and the wisdom to know the difference and act accordingly.) I was out of the habit of praying to connect with God. That was the moment I gave up the need to control and the need to know how everything would unfold.

I felt the power of divine love and I immediately made the decision to live in faith and love every day, moment by moment, fully in the present, to surrender in prayer and to begin to fully honor and trust my intuition. Something shifted in me and I felt peace. The present is indeed perfect and everything unfolds from that perfection.

Here are several examples of awakening experiences:

- Discovering the passion in your business as your calling to serve the world for the highest good
- Finding your soul mate and feeling truly happy and connected

after a painful relationship

- Feeling the void of child-rearing responsibilities; realizing you must get to know yourself and your spouse all over again or in new ways
- A serendipitous meeting or conversation which sparks an "aha" moment or a reminder of a dream you gave up on or have not allowed yourself to think about, let alone believe is still possible
- Waking from a dream, realizing that while you have happily chosen to nurture your family members, you have not felt fully alive. You want more from your relationships, your business, and your life
- Listening to a speaker at a meeting or conference, reading a book, listening to a radio show or television host, hearing a phrase or thought spoken by your priest, minister or rabbi that reminded you of a deep loving truth that touches your soul and awakens something in you
- Have you awoken to—and in—your life? Invest quiet time and invite your intuition to guide you to the answer. You will have a deep knowing.

Do you know what you truly want? If you are unsure, here are two ways to get that clarity:

1. Ask someone you trust to listen to you describe the deepest desires of your heart; this person is to speak the truth lovingly and be a sounding board for you; or,
2. Choose a time and place free of distractions. Use this time to reflect and write in your journal about your deepest desire(s) as if you knew you could have whatever it is you truly want. (Note: Don't worry or think about HOW it is possible. Just use your imagination, as a child would, to think about HOW IT LOOKS and HOW YOU FEEL about living your dream life).

JOURNAL ENTRY GUIDE #2

Use the space provided to write about what you think and feel when you ask yourself the questions: What do I truly want? How would I feel if I had that? What does it mean to me?

3. You explore and discover

Once you are awakened, you will have a burning desire to explore and experience more that feels real and authentic for you. At first you will feel very different because the experience is not the same as you're accustomed to. You will feel joy deep inside and you may not have words to describe it. Going back to the sleep state is not an option! You discover the joy within and you consciously choose thoughts, words and actions to continually experience that feeling of joy.

It may be scary for you if you still have excess baggage including feelings of unworthiness or patterns of self sabotage. This is when you must shed your excess baggage (more in Chapter 3) and where your support team can help.

When you choose actions that bring you more joy, you experience being your best and highest self; a feeling of being in the flow, or what my client Lilly describes as "flowing like a river". You recognize clues that confirm you are on track and lead you to the next steps in your divine journey. You begin to notice that with trust in your divine journey, everything unfolds effortlessly.

Following, I summarize my exploration and journey of discovery so you will be inspired and find an application to your own life.

My exploration sprung from two conscious choices:

1. The decision to trust and follow my intuition, and

2. To take action in my easy, joy-filled and inspired way, guided by my intuition; to be an instrument of God in my divine journey of making a difference in the world with my innate talents.

I paid attention to the actions that brought me joy and then repeated those actions. As a result, I made milestone discoveries and met amazing people.

I vividly remember when my exploration began and what I discovered about myself. It was just after listening to Father Claudio speak about being an instrument of God. After deciding that I wanted to find my soul purpose work, I prayed for divine guidance to what that might be. To this day I pray for divine guidance in all I do.

Coaching Business

Since committing to fully trusting my intuition, I took action to register for a self employment feasibility program. That led to meeting my first set of special coaches, Teresia LaRocque, Michael Walsh and Kevin Lawrence. I learned much more about coaching and then officially launched my coaching business. After coaching my first client I had a deep cellular knowing that I was to serve others through a coaching business. Following my intuition, I registered for coach training and graduated from Coach University. Later, I studied for behavioral and values assessment certification. Immersed in the coaching world, not only did I meet enlightened and service-oriented individuals on the world stage including Lance Secretan, but I saw what was extraordinary in the "ordinary" people with whom I crossed paths.

Evolving myself

Following my intuition, I invested in my next significant coach, Jean-Pierre LeBlanc, and made many discoveries.

These discoveries include my path to:

- natural well being (a more holistic approach to my health using pure essential oils and conscious awareness of my emotions),
- an improved relationship with my husband Richard (understanding male and female synergies and reconnecting with my feminine energy, greater acceptance of my responsibility to focus on the truth in all of my communications, rekindled passion, renewed commitment to our relationship), and
- the gift of reawakening my inner peace which I use to facilitate my own clients (I am more fully present to listen powerfully and role model and mirror truth, wisdom, and unconditional love).

Discovering the essence of me as pure love was humbling, as well as deeply joyful. With ease, I generously love my family and all with whom I cross paths.

Loving and Serving Others

Acting on the advice of a trusted friend, the late Douglas Jung, the first Chinese Canadian Member of Parliament, I joined the Burnaby Board of Trade. On invitation to chair and take their 2nd Business Excellence Awards gala to the next level, I was reminded of my gift of leadership.

That led to joining the world of Rotary and as a two-term president and current board member, I continue to use my leadership skills to serve both local and global communities.

Lance Secretan's description of Servant Leadership gave me the words to describe my leadership style in his book, "Inspire! What Great Leaders Do." It aligns with my discovery of love and service as my purpose and I used his process to identify my destiny statement.

Discovering the essence of who I am, my purpose and my destiny were part of the deep foundation of my life and business. I am forever thankful to my dynamic support team of loving family members and personal and business friends throughout my journey. I love them all deeply.

In summary, what I discovered is:

- God is centered in my life. Spiritual connection is vital for me
- My soul's purpose is to love and serve with my gifts
- My love and service is to my family, my business and my local and global communities.

What inspiration or "Aha" is there for you? Write it down.

Your Being Statement

Once you discover your core being or your essence, you have an important and forever guidance system. You always create from that place. You have the feel of Living Your Vacation every day.

What has worked for me and my clients is identifying a word or phrase that succinctly and effectively captures the Masterpiece that is you. Your word/phrase has special meaning to you, so don't worry about how it sounds to anyone else. Here are some examples to inspire you:

I'm pure love	I help everyone win
I'm amazing joy	I am authentic and want the best for all
Brilliant Star	Effortless people connector
One with the universe	Open hearted warrior
Compassionate and Loving	Elegance and grace
I care deeply with a keen eye for details	Gentle and kind to people, animals and the environment

Take the time to write what you discover about yourself. You will discover clues from what you notice about yourself, your patterns, your accomplishments, what others have told you and what you love about yourself. Consider investing in the services of a personal coach who possesses a self-knowing, listens attentively to who you are, and effortlessly expresses your soul's voice as a mirror for your benefit.

Objective but caring feedback is helpful when you recognize that it enhances what you already know to accomplish whatever you choose.

Discovering who you are gives you so much joy that you always choose to be your highest and best self. With focused attention on being loving, feeling loved, and experiencing harmony, your life unfolds in a pure, focused fashion so you live each day with effortless ease.

> *"When we harness the forces of harmony, joy & love, we create success and good fortune with effortless ease."* — DEEPAK CHOPRA

Following is an example of what I discovered about myself and how I embraced my own life. I share it so that it can be a catalyst for your own discovery.

The anchor or lighthouse in my life journey is the knowing of who I am. I am pure love. My faith, born of love and inspired by my mother is my solid foundation. I am loved unconditionally. I love unconditionally. Therefore my intention and approach to everything and everyone is pure and creates winning circumstances for all, in all ways.

I value spiritual connection to God and to people; family, friends, clients, my Rotary family, my community and my fellow human beings. My purpose is to be of service as a successful, powerful healer and my destiny is to empower others to create a more peaceful and loving world.

My business aligns with who I am as a reflection of my life; my business is my calling to serve the world. Discovering this integration of my business with my life allows me to address priorities in the different aspects of my life with purpose and faith.

When you know at a soul level who you are, remember on a daily basis who you are, and consciously make decisions from that place, you know the joy of living your vacation. You feel an ease and purposefulness every day. This quotation from Neale Donald Walsch resonates with me and I want to share it with you as you clarify who you are:

> *"Every decision you make—every decision—is not a decision about what to do. It's a decision about Who You Are. When you see this, when you understand it, everything changes. You begin to see life in a new way. All events, occurrences, and situations turn into opportunities to do what you came here to do."*

It is vital to explore all aspects of your life—personal, spiritual, financial and business/work. Make your discoveries and assess alignment to who you are with the vision you hold in each area. Celebrate what is working for you and positively address what is not working.

JOURNAL ENTRY GUIDES #3 & #4

Entry #3: Brainstorm to discover your Being Statement. Describe what you know about yourself. Identify your essence and ask others who know you. Determine if that feels complete and which next action is appropriate based on your discovery. Check your inner guidance.

Entry # 4: Assess where you are in each aspect of your life and business/work to appreciate what is working and to clarify which actions serve your highest purpose.

The journey of discovery is unique to you; I did it with the support of coaches. Explore and identify the best coach for you to support you on this purposeful journey.

Asking for help and having *your* ideal support team are significant components in successfully designing your life. (More in Chapter 3.)

Your life and business, or work, do not define you.

Let me repeat: Your life and business, or work, do not define you.

Who you are is reflected in your approach to your life, your business and your work. Enjoy your journey of discovery!

Who you really are is a Masterpiece, connected to other masterpieces.

You See Who Others Are

This is your relationship with you and others.

> *"No man is an Island, entire of itself; every man is a piece of the Continent, a part of the main."* — JOHN DONNE

> *"...love thy neighbor as thyself."* — ROMANS 13:9

You are not alone. You are meant to live in collaboration and harmony with others and to be of service to each other. For your relationships to thrive, you are called to be your highest self and see others at their highest selves, even when their behavior is not their best.

By making this shift to be your highest and best self and to see others as their highest and best selves, you will radically and powerfully alter the experiences of your life and experience true transformation. What if every day you chose to see the highest and best selves of those in your personal and business lives? What difference would that make to how you feel about yourself, others, and the results you experience?

The spiritual perspective of who you are, and choosing to see the masterpiece in others, requires you to raise your standards to that level. It will not always be easy. Do not worry if it does not feel natural at first; as long as you begin with a conscious decision, it will become easier with practice. It will become effortless; not thinking about it but naturally living it.

People provide great mirrors for us, often unknowingly. Once you discover who you are, you must nurture that knowledge with daily connection to the divine so you can more easily shine your brilliance.

Harmony with others begins with harmony within you. We all have something in common—to share in our humanity—and we are all connected. In your dream life, you are at your best and highest self in harmony with others. When you see the masterpiece in others, you will more easily connect with them at a deeper level.

To raise your standards, you must first recognize the barriers to seeing the masterpiece in others. You may unknowingly create barriers to enjoying amazing relationships; barriers developed from what you have learned and believe about yourself and others. Let's take a closer look at the areas of your life that contain the greatest opportunities to experience transformations. Barriers block the way to truly seeing others and therefore prevent the development of your relationships. Common barriers include:

Judgments

- When you spend energy judging yourself for mistakes you have made or for any fall short of your own or others' expectations, you are so focused on yourself that you do not have room to see the masterpiece in others

- When you judge others because they fall short of your expectations, you cannot see who they are but instead have imposed upon them what is not true.

Labels

- When you label others, you may have *some* accurate information but you are applying characteristics of a group to an individual which may not be accurate. That blinds you to the truth of the person.

Biases

- Regardless of the source of your bias, like labeling, your bias is not the truth of the other. You do not see the masterpiece in that person. Instead, your perception of the person is inaccurate and you make assumptions that prevent nourishment of your relationship.

Previous Experiences

- Assuming you have decided to remain in a specific personal or business relationship, your previous experiences may prevent the full enjoyment of your connection. Past experiences may be unresolved such as incomplete closures, resentments about the results of what you perceived to have occurred or not occurred, or anyone you have not forgiven for being wronged in some way.

Now is the perfect time to identify your barriers to seeing the masterpiece—or what is sacred—in the people in your life. Gain more clarity by listing them in your journal and brainstorm to find a statement that accurately describes how you approach every relationship. Below is my example for you to explore the simple and meaningful ways you can choose to perceive others.

I discovered the masterpiece in myself and I automatically acknowledge the masterpiece in others. This is a natural, clean and simple way for me to approach everyone.

JOURNAL ENTRY GUIDE #5

List your barriers to seeing the masterpiece in others and brainstorm your statement to approach and resolve every connection.

JOURNAL ENTRY GUIDE #6

Also, list those people with whom you want amazing relationships, both in your personal and professional lives. Identify what you want to experience in each relationship and the action steps you will take towards making that real, so that you enjoy deeply satisfying relationships.

Because we are all connected at a spiritual level, when we see the masterpiece in ourselves and in others, our lives are transformed to one of inner peace, joy and love. Living in this energy of love is *Living Your Vacation* and your dream life every day. Consider the power of your choices when you take action as described in the following Peace Prayer of St. Francis.

When I listened to James Twyman, the Peace Troubadour, sing and performed this live, I was moved to tears. Each of us has the capacity to be an instrument of peace. Read the following, and identify what resonates for you and the inspiration that results from the resonance.

The Peace Prayer of St. Francis

— By an anonymous Norman c. 1915 A.D.
Peace Prayer, **www.franciscan-archive.org**

Lord, make me an instrument of your peace.
Where there is hatred,
Let me sow love;
Where there is injury, pardon;
Where there is error, truth;
Where there is doubt, faith;
Where there is despair, hope;
Where there is darkness, light;
And where there is sadness, Joy.

O Divine Master grant that I may not so much
seek to be consoled
as to console;
To be understood, as to understand;
To be loved, as to love.
For it is in giving that we receive,
It is in pardoning that we are pardoned,
And it is in dying that we are born to eternal life.

CHAPTER 2

Every Day Can Be a Vacation

Define Your Destination

"Begin with the end in mind." — STEPHEN COVEY

ONCE YOU COMPLETE THE STEPS IN YOUR INWARD journey to discover Who You Are and Your Perception of Others, it's time to take a closer look at your dream life. Your dream life is about what you truly want to experience from the depths of your soul.

The same clarity you have in deciding the destination of your vacation is the same clarity you need to create your dream life.

Here are a few questions to assess where you are along the journey:

- Have you been on 'auto-pilot', busy with your daily activities without a clear and purposeful vision of where you are going?
- Are there days when your business is not going the way you want it to, doubts creep in, others reaffirm your doubts and you forget that it is your calling to serve the world?
- Do you compare yourself with others and ignore your intuition to trust your unique way of making a difference in the world through your life and your business?
- Are your relationships not as enjoyable and fulfilling as you envision?

If you've answered "Yes" to any of these questions, this is a reminder for you to connect with —and clarify —your vision and use spiritual wisdom daily to guide you.

Most likely you have a deep knowing that you are on your divine path. When you are "in the flow" and actively living your vision, you have inner peace and harmony, are at ease in your daily actions, are happy about your relationships, and are thus making a difference in the world, easily attracting new customers and friends. This is what it's like when you connect with, and express, your soul's passion and purpose. Naturally, prosperity follows in surprising ways, which you will consciously acknowledge and appreciate.

When you live according to your highest vision, your soul's passion and purpose are authentically expressed. And when you are authentic, you radiate peace, harmony, and joy, inspiring others along the way. You feel on purpose with your business. Your life is soul satisfying. When you express who you are in your most genuine and easy way, your soul sings and you profoundly affect others by being and doing what you love. Your vision must guide you on a loving journey that inspires integrity in all areas of business and life.

One important reminder: You deserve to have your dream life. What you truly want is the life of your dreams and to experience the feeling that you are on vacation every day.

Let's "begin with the end in mind" and define your dream vision for your life and work.

Your Life Vision

When I talk with clients, friends, business associates and family members about their ideal vacation, the following summarizes what they shared: They most want the feeling of being stress-free, relaxed yet excited, full of joy, passionate and purposeful in what they do, and doing whatever they want, whenever they want and with the people who mean the most to them.

During those moments is when you feel joy that is deep within you. You are naturally your best and highest self.

Here are some ideas about living your dream life:

- you are at your best and highest self
- everything flows easily
- you are loved and love unconditionally
- you are unconcerned about money
- your projects are completed or are on target
- you have no unresolved issues
- you take nothing personally
- what you think, say or do is respectful and with good intentions for all
- you do only what inspires you
- you do everything in an inspiring way
- every day feels like a vacation day
- you and your family enjoy optimal health
- you feel vibrantly alive
- you radiate peace, joy and confidence
- you attract only the best people and opportunities
- you generously give your time, talent and resources
- you are self-fulfilled
- you see and appreciate the blessings in your life.

Therefore, to live your vacation is to live your dream life every day because every day feels like a vacation day.

Your Life Vision Statement

Your Life Vision Statement communicates clearly and succinctly what you most want for your life. It describes your deepest desire and is compelling enough to pull you forward; it is a powerful guide when you need it most. It serves your highest interest to keep it alive by regularly reminding yourself of it.

Write your Life Vision Statement.

While yours will be unique to you, use the following examples as your inspiration:

- I am at peace with myself and everyone in my life
- My Life flows like a river
- My Life is passionately creative and expansive
- My Life is a legacy of Love
- I am fully alive and savor all my experiences
- I am vibrantly healthy and inspire others to live a healthy lifestyle.

JOURNAL ENTRY GUIDE #7

Complete the following: *My Life Vision Statement is:*

Your Business/Work Vision

During my coaching sessions with clients, this is what they say on the topic of desired business or work vision: In business, everything is in order. Files are organized; data is stored and backed up. Systems are in place. Every role is clearly defined. Feedback is welcome at all levels of leadership. Everyone is well-compensated. Relationships are valued and honored. Teams are high functioning, effective and fully engaged. Giving back to the community is included in budgets and participation in charitable community events is encouraged. Customers are satisfied and they share their experiences with potential customers; ideal customers are so much fun and a joy to serve.

Here are some ideas about living your dream life in your business or work:

- You are passionate about the work you do.
- Your talents and strengths are fully expressed regularly and rewarded consistently.
- Systems are in place in all areas of your business or in your position.
- Conversations are heart-based and the richness of diversity is enjoyed and appreciated.
- Challenges are attended to calmly, respectfully, with the priority being people; there are solutions and wins for everyone.
- Teamwork, creativity, co-operation, and leadership are valued.
- Everyone feels listened to and heard.

Your Business/Work Vision Statement

Write your business or work vision statement. It aligns with who you are and is a reflection of your best and highest self at work; contributing and making a difference in the world. Here are some Business/ Work Vision Statements to get you started on defining yours:

- Your success is my business
- Delivering quality products and exceptional service is our commitment every day
- I partner with others to consistently exceed expectations
- My work reflects 100% quality effort
- We care for each other and the environment.

JOURNAL ENTRY GUIDE #8

Complete the following: *My Business/Work Vision Statement is:*

Your Daily Commitments

Your commitment is key to your success. If commitment seems scary to you, it may be because you feel it restricts you, or gets in the way of your creativity or freedom. Now is the perfect time to consider what it *really* does for you.

When you make a commitment and honor it, you have a focus for your attention. That focused attention means you have given yourself the permission to be free from anything that is a distraction from your commitment. Since whatever you place your attention on expands, you will have positive results. You will in fact, in the commitment, experience the *most* freedom because you come from a place of choice to first make the commitment and thereafter choose thoughts, words and behaviors that align with that commitment.

Using myself as an example, I am a conscious entrepreneur, and a Rotarian, committed to making a home cooked meal on a daily basis for my family.

When I made those commitments, I actually accessed my creativity, became more organized and felt joy and satisfaction in making time for my business, volunteering as a Rotarian and honoring the commitment to my family. I felt most free as I made conscious loving choices.

Your Compelling Commitment Statement

Connect with the deep joy you experience when you honor your commitment to the highest vision of what you want. These gifts of joy, waiting for you as a result of honoring your daily commitment, will transform your life beyond measure.

Some days you may lose sight of your dream vision or you may lose sight of who you are. Don't be discouraged. These are the times to remind yourself of your commitment. Depending on what is happening in your life at the moment, a specific Compelling Commitment Statement describing the vision of one aspect of your life or business may just be what you need.

For example, health challenges, a failed marriage, loss of work or a change of career means a commitment to a new related vision such as:

- I am committed to an active and healthy lifestyle
- I am committed to experiencing a joy filled, fun and harmonious marriage
- I am committed to a loving and meaningful relationship with my children, as my first priority
- I am committed to meaningful and profitable work
- I am committed to the highest ethical standards in my life and career
- I am committed to going out with my college age daughter or son once a month, no matter what
- I am committed to be unconditionally constructive and kind in all my communications
- I am committed to stopping, breathing and counting to 10 before responding to any situation brought to my attention
- I am committed to scheduling one day a week just for me
- I am committed to going to bed by 10 PM every weekday
- I am committed to maintaining the romance in my relationship
- I am committed to consistently donating 10% of my income to worthy causes.

This commitment statement must be compelling to you. You must feel the joy of the results you want to experience. This will pull you forward. When you are off track, you will more quickly get back on track when you remind yourself of what you most want.

For many people, I realize that a commitment might not be something that gets you really excited. Speaking from experience,

I have developed an 8-step process that helps you not only make commitments and keep them but really celebrate the commitments in your life.

A point to note is that making and keeping commitments are the keys to experiencing more freedom in your life. So, let me show you the 8-step process to help you gain clarity and celebrate your commitments to move forward so you can live your vacation every day:

1. Stop and take a few deep breaths, remembering who you are.

Stopping for just a moment or two everyday to take a few deep breaths allows you to get grounded or centered. This is the greatest gift you can give yourself as one of the things you do most while on vacation is relax and take deep breaths.

With the thousands of thoughts bombarding you throughout the day, it is important to be in a place of calm and feel centered to allow your best and highest self to emerge and be present. Taking a few deep breaths does wonders to connect with your physical body. So do this every day of your life. Then think of your Being Statement to remind you of your essential nature; who you are, a masterpiece with gifts to share.

2. Acknowledge how you feel and where you are in life.

Accept whatever you feel as human. Feelings are neither good nor bad; they just are. Acknowledge your feelings without judgment. This is important, as judgments slow you down, distract or overwhelm you, or keep you stuck. Once you acknowledge them, truthfully assess where you are. If you are going on vacation, you cannot get to your destination until you know your starting point, otherwise the map does not make any sense. Similarly in your life, stop, acknowledge how you feel, without judgment get clear on where you are and find something to appreciate. From that place you are ready to take the next step to move forward. Remind yourself that it is part of your divine path in your divine journey.

3. Write your heart-based Compelling Commitment Statement.

With the acceptance of how you feel and where you are, reveal your deepest desire and write your Compelling Commitment Statement. Once you are ready to begin your vacation, you know how excited you feel when you think of actually being on vacation. And so it is in your everyday life when you are clear about —and connect with —what your heart desires. You feel a deep joy that energizes you to move forward. Having this Compelling Commitment Statement reminds you of what's really important in your life and gives you a boost when you most need it. Rewrite or review your Compelling Commitment Statement, if you already have one.

4. Identify blockages and the choice(s) you have.

As you know, in your daily life everything does not always go as planned. Sometimes you run into the proverbial brick wall. What gets in the way are your fears and doubts of ever getting what you truly want, and not seeing clearly how you will get what you really want. Other thoughts you may have that get in the way include being overly concerned about what others think or say, learned habits that undermine your self confidence, limiting beliefs of which you are unaware and have not asked for feedback, etc. The choice you always have is the perspective you take. This means you can choose the thoughts, words and actions that align with your commitment and ask someone to help you be accountable for —and celebrate —your commitments. When you make conscious choices, you empower yourself. By choosing to honor your commitments you will feel a deep sustainable joy and live your vacation every day.

5. Identify what and who will support you.

Knowing yourself will help you to identify what supports you. You are not alone; there are people who will gladly help you, if you ask. If you are going on a vacation, you either ask a travel agent or frequent traveler friend for help, or you do your own research by getting brochures or searching the web. The same applies to your life. Knowing who and what will support you in celebrating your commitments and making sure you make space to have them included in your life, will add to the ease and joy you experience every day. There are people who show up, sometimes unexpectedly, when in faith you pray, meditate or however you make your connection with what you know to be the highest source of power. Identify the people who can support you. Daily spiritual practices engage the joy you are capable of experiencing every day.

6. Identify what actions you need to take.

Making a commitment and taking action will get you the results you want and so much more. Most of the time, you may know clearly or have a hunch as to what actions will get you the results you want. It is important now to set up a customized system to make sure you identify all necessary actions, all the people who can help, when you plan to accomplish the goals and the accountability structure that works best for you. The system and accountability structure is there to support your follow-through. Choose a friend, life partner, business partner or a professional coach with whom you can connect regularly. This makes the process more enjoyable and increases your chances of following through on your commitment to take action. Two important criteria: 1. Each action should be inspiring or should contain an element of inspiration to follow through on each action and, 2. Each action is to be done in YOUR easy and inspired way of getting it done, not necessarily how others do it.

A point to note here: Unexpected or new action steps may present themselves after you have taken a predetermined action step. Be open and flexible to integrate those new types of action steps.

7. Take action, one step at a time.

Sometimes, what may seem like too many actions can be overwhelming, so identifying the very next step is a great way to make progress. Just Begin.

> *"Whatever you can do or dream you can, begin it. Boldness has genius, power and magic in it. Begin it now!"*
>
> — JOHANN WOLFGANG VON GOETHE

If you are unsure, ask your intuition and pay attention to clues that show up. A point to note: When you do not follow through, whether there is a pattern or not, don't beat yourself up; proceed to explore what help you need. Pay attention, trust your hunches/intuition and follow your inner guidance. Trusting your intuition becomes easier with practice, raising your awareness of its power to serve you and the good of all.

8. Celebrate each step.

Make it a habit to celebrate each step you take. This last step is by no means the least important step. In fact it is a *necessary* step to celebrate your commitment and to increase the joy you feel every day. It is often an overlooked action step. Some reasons it is overlooked include:

- Celebrating isn't a developed habit
- The belief that you only celebrate when you have a major accomplishment
- The thought that celebration costs too much money
- The lack of awareness of the value of celebrating even the smallest of accomplishments.

Celebrating every step gives you joy every time. It may be as simple as sharing it with a family member, a friend, a colleague or your coach. The joy you feel in celebrating will energize you and each subsequent step will flow more easily and quickly.

Living Your Vacation means deciding to savor JOY NOW.

JOURNAL ENTRY GUIDE #9

Use the journal to record about each step of the process above and write your Compelling Commitment Statement. Refer to the information regularly as a guide to celebrate each action step.

CHAPTER 3

Travel Light: What to Leave Behind... and What to Bring Along

HAVE YOU TRAVELLED WITH A LOT OF LUGGAGE AS well as with little luggage to notice the difference in how you feel when you travel light? Coming from a place of conscious choice-making and taking full responsibility, traveling light in your life is about ridding yourself of excess baggage and taking along what truly inspires and supports you on your journey. These are two strategies I use and recommend to my clients:

1. *Shed your excess baggage*
2. *Take only essentials with you.*

These will help you to be more energized and experience successful results as you live, work and manifest with ease.

You may ask: What does shedding excess baggage and taking along only essentials have to do with manifesting?

Well, let's first define "manifest."

Merriam-Webster Dictionary defines manifest as:

1. *readily perceived by the senses and especially by the sight*
2. *easily understood or recognized by the mind.*

Now, let's say what you manifest or see in physical form or is recognized by your mind are results affected by your actions. Your actions are therefore very powerful. A springboard to, or fuel for, your actions, is your attitude, your perspective, your beliefs, and your mindset.

While the fuel for your actions has been formed or developed in various ways—some conscious and some unconscious—your first powerful action step is to become more aware and conscious in your actions. That is where you can make choices, create, and take full responsibility.

So, to manifest or see more of what you want, you must consciously take action from your highest and best self. Your highest and best self will be present when you are free of the burdens of excess baggage and you use what will support you to be your highest and best self; your essentials. Now, it IS still possible to manifest some of what you want while carrying excess baggage. However, it will not be easy or sustainable.

After discovering who you are and clarifying what you want in your dream life, from a place of awareness and choice it is now time to prepare for the most enjoyable journey with as much ease as possible. Remember that whatever occurs is part of your divine journey, but *you can choose to travel light.*

Please take note of a few important reminders: You were born a masterpiece. Your best and highest self shows up with ease when you are connected to your source and are free of anything or anyone you allow to weigh you down or drain your energy.

You probably noticed I said, "You allow." Yes I did.

When you choose this perspective of awareness and acceptance, you see the difference it makes to you, those around you and the results you experience. It empowers you to take action and move away from blaming to assuming full responsibility for your contribution to every situation.

Let's take a closer look at each of these two life-transforming strategies.

• STRATEGY 1 •
Shed Your Excess Baggage – Identify, Release, Create

In every area of your life you may be carrying excess baggage. In the following paragraphs, I will address the main areas of life; Personal, Spiritual, Financial and Business. Feel free to add other key areas when you do the exercises.

To make it tangible and relevant to you, I recommend a 3-step process to manifest with ease within each of the main areas. Let me first define the term to help you understand the significance of shedding your "excess baggage."

Define Excess Baggage

Excess baggage is that which is not necessary or essential, heavy and not necessarily useful, delays you from moving forward as quickly as you want, and may even be harmful.

Your excess baggage are like balls and chains attached to you, preventing you or your business from moving forward naturally, lightly, and freely. They are also like holes draining your healthy, vibrant, and joyful energy.

With excess baggage, you feel tired, weighed down, not fully alive, not reminding yourself to do that which gives you deep joy. You may feel stuck and overwhelmed, procrastinating on the actions most important and meaningful for you.

When you travel light on a daily basis, you live, work, and manifest with ease. You will also be more likely to have optimal health and be energized to live passionately with a sense of purpose.

Imagine carrying around excess weight, which you do not see but you feel a heaviness in every part of you, that is weighing you down (you may be carrying excess physical weight as well). Understandably you feel tired. You may have ways to temporarily energize yourself but you don't feel energized for long because the holes are draining as quickly or more quickly than you can replenish or reenergize yourself.

Let's examine what this means for you.

Personal Excess Baggage

Your personal excess baggage robs you of energy and creates obstacles to living the dream life you are meant to live. They also create stress which leads to ill health.

• STEP 1 •
Identify Your Personal Excess Baggage

Use the following examples to help you identify your personal excess baggage.

These are:

- all your incompletes; e.g. projects started, routine and recreational activities in the back of your mind and not honored
- resentments and feelings of being wronged in the past
- guilty feelings of mistakes, unworthiness or unhealed wounds
- judgments of yourself and others based on expectations
- places of being stuck and feeling overwhelmed
- tolerations of clutter inside and outside your home
- unresolved matters with family and friends
- limiting beliefs about yourself and your capabilities or about others
- dramatic and pain-filled stories of past experiences and negative anticipation of the future
- disappointments about yourself and about others
- failed relationships

- unexpressed needs and desires
- not making time for fun and what fills you with joy
- what you automatically say "Yes" to that is best done by others
- tolerating ill health and not honoring your desire for a healthy lifestyle.

What are your personal excess baggage items? Identify one area to shed and take appropriate action.

• STEP 2 •

What do you want to release to shed your personal excess baggage?

Some of what gets in the way of shedding your excess baggage includes the following, which you can use to determine your next step:

- Your need to be right
- Fear of what you think will happen or what others will say
- Your mistaken assumption that it will change your essential nature
- You are familiar with what your life looks like now and you are unsure or worried about the unknown of what change will occur
- Your fear that past negative experiences will be repeated
- Your feelings of guilt
- Your limiting beliefs about what you deserve to have or are capable of having
- Your automatic habit of giving negative meaning to occurrences or other people's actions.

What are you willing to release so you can shed your personal excess baggage?

• STEP 3 •

What do you want to create in this area of your personal life?

With the space available from shedding excess baggage, you have room to create what you truly want in living your vacation every day.

Go back to Chapter 2. Review your Life Vision Statement and your Compelling Commitment Statement. Review them for alignment with what you want to create to replace each excess baggage item you shed.

Here are some examples to inspire you to get clear on what you want to create:

- Harmony in a particular relationship or all your relationships
- More fun and recreation, scheduled regularly
- Extreme self care as a priority
- New habits to feel fully alive that mirror a healthy lifestyle
- Your inspired success formula
- The courage and inspiration to freely, fully, powerfully, and authentically express who you are.

What do you want to create in your personal life?

To explain this more clearly, let me share what happened with a client.

His biggest area of excess baggage was holding onto a secret of wasting family finances and not letting his wife know, for fear she would leave him. This excess baggage—with other resentments—negatively affected his health. He used sleeping pills to sleep, was unusually short tempered with his family, was asleep to his identity and had an unclear direction in life. What was certain was the love from his family members, his love for his wife, kids, and extended family members and his desire for harmony.

By becoming more aware that he was carrying excess baggage, the negative impact it had on his life, the fears that held him back, the truth of who he is and the power he had to shed them, he made a difficult but meaningful decision to share his truth. Shedding one significant challenging issue, made it easier to move forward to the next step in truth and love. He saw more clearly and affirmed that he wanted to create more joy, to continue to discover himself and to continue moving in a positive, healthy direction.

JOURNAL ENTRY GUIDE #10

Use the journal to record the answers to your **personal life** questions in each of the three steps above. Identify the support you need and how you will celebrate your efforts.

Spiritual Excess Baggage

When you are connected with your highest source, you have the faith and power to see solutions, opportunities, and possibilities more clearly. Your self fulfillment, enlightenment and inspiration are more likely to manifest every day.

You may have a deep knowing that something is missing in living a meaningful life. When you reconnect or connect with your highest source and see your connection with others, you also see that whatever you do has an impact on you, everyone around you, and the world. If the memories of past experiences prevent you from embracing your spirituality, now is the time for you to connect with your highest source of power. Your divine journey will feel much lighter and you will have direct access to the most powerful source to live your dream life every day.

Let's take a look at how this applies to you.

• STEP 1 •
Identify Your Spiritual Excess Baggage

The following are examples of where you may carry excess baggage:

- Spiritual baggage might be the load you carry about a particular religion or person. You may have given up on your spirituality and yearn for that connection, whether or not it is with an organized group that shares your beliefs
- You may have been disappointed with the way a particular situation was handled and you stopped attending religious services. You may have stopped practicing your faith because of unresolved resentments or because of a change in your life situation
- You are afraid or have given up on your desire to connect to a deeper part of yourself.

Whatever the reason, if you now feel a void and a yearning to reconnect with your faith or a spiritual source, be it God or whatever supports you the best, honor that internal nudge you feel. With loving energy for the good of all, it is time to take action and not waste another minute without experiencing spiritual well being.

Just decide and take the next step. That next step might be to explore a spiritual community where you will thrive or to recommit to daily habits of prayer, meditation or periods of silence.

What is your spiritual excess baggage? Identify one area and take action.

• STEP 2 •
What do you want to release to shed your spiritual excess baggage?

Some of what prevents you from shedding your excess baggage may include the following, which you can use to determine your next step:

- Your limiting belief that it is too hard or impossible for change to happen
- Your generalizations and negative view of people within your spiritual or religious groups
- Your busy lifestyle with no room for anything else
- Your fear of what is unknown and unfamiliar
- Your limited view of spirituality.

What are you ready to release to help you shed your spiritual excess baggage?

• STEP 3 •

What do you want to create in this area of your spiritual life?

Once you shed your spiritual excess baggage, you will have room to create what you want to develop in your spirituality.

Your spiritual life is individual to you. Here are some examples of what you can create in your spirituality:

- Daily spiritual practice, e.g. prayers, meditation, quiet time in nature
- Gratitude prayers as a family
- Attend regular church services or meetings of your faith
- Learn about other religions or religious practices in the world
- Be kinder to yourself and to others as a way of being
- Respect for all life
- Volunteer time regularly to help those in need
- Simplify your life and discover who you really are. Be true to yourself and others
- Seek enlightenment, peace, joy and harmony.

What do you want to create in your spiritual life?

This is an example of what happened with a client whose spiritual baggage was the regret she carried for years. She experienced great pain caused by leaving her husband who loved her and provided well for her.

While she moved on with her life, she was not completely healed because she had not forgiven herself. She also felt God had not forgiven her. This regret showed up in self sabotage actions as she did not feel she deserved what she really wanted.

The costs were high as she sacrificed a deeper level of love in her next marriage. With the loving support of family members and a deep yearning to live on purpose and remain connected to God, she made a commitment to embark on an inward journey of self discovery, be true to herself and to give generously to others.

It felt like a ton of emotional excess baggage lifted when she forgave herself, committed to being kind and loving to herself, began taking great care of herself, and recommitted to her desire to honor all her relationships. As a bonus, she got on track to shedding physical weight as well.

JOURNAL ENTRY GUIDE #11

Use your journal to record the answers to your **spiritual life** questions in each of the three steps above. Identify the support you need and how you will celebrate your efforts.

Financial Excess Baggage

When you manage your financial commitments and have an abundant perspective, you see the wealth you do have and where your attention needs to be focused. Your inner peace with money and placing attention on a system to have your finances handled means you are free to focus on being and doing what you are meant to do as a contributor to a better world.

Focusing on money *alone* is a distraction from the greater truth of the abundance you already have and are capable of achieving. Do you limit yourself with beliefs about the scarcity of money and how difficult it is to earn it?

If you answer "Yes," when you shed that excess baggage and replace your attention with gratitude for the abundance you do have, your shift in perspective and energy will increase the opportunities for your financial well being.

In the beginning, I know it is difficult to shift your attention to gratitude when what you see is apparent lack. This difficulty is based in habit; you have many years of experience in seeing what you do not have. Choosing to shift your attention to the blessings in your life requires a conscious choice and it is a new habit which becomes easier with practice. I promise.

Let's take a look at how this applies to you.

• STEP 1 •
Identify Your Financial Excess Baggage

You will recognize excess baggage by noticing where you have strong emotions around money. Your sense of inner peace is affected and you make decisions based *solely* on money. Your financial excess baggage may include any of the following:

- Holding on to learned limiting beliefs of not having enough, so regardless of how much money you actually have, there isn't a peaceful satisfaction of abundance but instead one of scarcity and fear that money will run out
- Your self worth is excessively tied to how much money you have at the moment

- The only strategy you adopt is to "save for a rainy day" and while you may be consistently investing a percentage of your income, you constantly worry about and expect rainy days and cannot enjoy what you have.
- You have not created a system to put healthy consistent attention on your money and are vague about your financial position.
- Not having enough money consumes your attention and you feel guilty about not contributing to areas of your life such as treating yourself well, tithing to your church, helping others in need, etc.

What is your financial excess baggage? Identify one area and take action.

• STEP 2 •

What do you want to release in order to shed your financial excess baggage?

Once you have identified your financial excess baggage items, your next step is to know what prevents you from shedding them. The following are examples of what might be weighing you down and preventing you from shedding your financial excess baggage:

- Habitual attention on not having enough
- Excessive fears of future "rainy days"
- Fear of looking more closely at your finances and honestly assessing where you are
- Your self worth is directly related to money
- Having an abundance of money and spirituality cannot coexist beautifully.

What will you release to help you shed your financial excess baggage?

• STEP 3 •
What do you want to create in this area of your financial well being?

When you shed your financial excess baggage, you will have increased energy to be more creative in fully using your talents, be more open to possibilities, see more options and enjoy the difference you are making. Imagine the possibilities of placing attention on sharing your talents and seeing that your finances are handled with ease! The following are examples of what to create in areas of your financial well-being:

- Freedom to pamper yourself and all your loved ones
- A sustainable system to help others share their talents
- A legacy of conscious leaders and families enriching each others' lives
- Significant financial support of causes for which you are passionate
- Explore a dream you had forgotten about but still have a desire to manifest.

What will you release to shed your financial excess baggage and make room to be creative and manifest your dreams?

Here is an example of a client's fears and her focus on what could happen after retirement.

This fear showed up often and got in the way of her ability to see that in fact she did have investments in place to secure her retirement. Her fears were based on years of believing that "rainy days" would always be ahead. Her fears clouded her memory of the abundant experiences she already experienced. The cost to her was the absence of deep joy. She had much to celebrate based on all the dreams she had already manifested. Her life was absolutely amazing. While she knew that on some level, being aware of the baggage and shedding it helped her to see how wealthy she actually is. During challenging times, she reminds herself of all of her blessings, her courage and strength and her many accomplishments, and she gives herself permission to take extremely great care of herself and to trust the wisdom of her heart.

JOURNAL ENTRY GUIDE #12

Use the journal to record the answers to your **financial** questions in each of the three steps above. Identify the support you need and how you will celebrate your efforts.

Business Excess Baggage

When your business is free of excess baggage, everything runs smoothly. The results are productivity, effectiveness, high performance and profitability.

As a business owner and leader, your personal excess baggage negatively impacts your business. If what you want is a thriving, growing, and profitable business it is well worth your investment of resources to assess your personal excess baggage and the business excess baggage that is hindering productivity and effectiveness of everyone on your team.

Let's take a closer look at how this applies to your business.

• STEP 1 •
Identify Your Business Excess Baggage

Here are several examples of how the weight of excess baggage shows up in your business:

- Little or no awareness of the impact of personal excess baggage and a strategy and plan to manage it
- Ineffective communication habits
- Lack of, or outdated, systems to facilitate everyone in succeeding in their various roles
- No effective or measurable feedback system to improve and evaluate each person's contribution, strengths, and areas for improvement
- Ineffective & uninspired leadership
- Fear of communicating truth
- Limiting beliefs that there are only winners or losers in any negotiation, and managers and staff cannot successfully collaborate to create win-win-wins
- Lack of effective systems to manage all areas of your business
- Lack of collective team efforts and approaches for getting things done
- Outdated and poorly maintained equipment
- Unused inventory or equipment, unnecessary files, books, magazines, clutter
- Excessive time spent with non ideal customers.

What are the excess baggage items relating to your business? Identify one area and take appropriate action.

• STEP 2 •
What do you want to release to shed excess baggage in your business?

Like all other areas of excess baggage, those in your business have been there for various reasons and served a purpose. Now that you are ready to take your business to the next level, you want to make room by supporting what it takes to shed all excess baggage.

Following are examples of what you can choose to release to ensure successful shedding of excess baggage:

- Fear of making big changes or any change at all
- Limiting beliefs of having to figure things out for yourself
- Fear of not having all the answers and revealing your vulnerability
- Not knowing exactly how everything will unfold
- Judgments about people's capacity to be resilient and find creative solutions just because it has not surfaced before or because of past mistakes
- Not trusting your inner knowing and the clues in front of you
- Fear of not having enough resources
- Reliance solely on what's tangibly outside of you and ignoring the intangible power within you.

What are you willing to release to shed your business excess baggage?

• STEP 3 •

What do you want to create in this area of your business?

Over time, you may have forgotten why and what you wanted to create in your business based on your original vision. If so, now is the time to reflect and reconnect with what you want to create. Here are some examples to get you started:

- A sustainable and thriving business that positively impact lives for generations to come
- A high functioning team with less of you operationally and more of you strategically
- Focus on everyone's strengths
- Collaborative, cohesive team working environment
- Systems to improve efficiency in all areas
- Caring, fun and inspired working environment in which everyone is valued and each member is free to express the innate

leaders they are

- Automation with practical and efficient systems allowing everyone's best work to shine brilliantly
- Strategic partnerships and joint ventures to provide the best results for all
- Development plans customized for each person
- Profitable growth for everyone's dream life.

What do you want to create in your business?

Here is an example of how a client shedding excess baggage both in her personal and business lives made a significant difference in the results she experienced.

Personal baggage shed included a realization of her own uninspired behaviors and unrecognized self worth, an understanding of family members' destructive behaviors, emotional clutter impacting time and space at home.

Business items shed included piles of business files all over the office floor and desks, and items that were difficult to find when needed. Systems were overwhelmed with growth of business. Lack of effective systems to address the administrative and financial details were among several time consuming tasks that drained her creative energy.

Taking the time to reorganize the business files and tools so everything had a "home" made them easily accessible. Investing in updated systems increased workflow and working more effectively with a professional bookkeeper were among the items that lifted business baggage. As a result, her efforts were maximized. There was a significant increase in business and ideal clients. With this growth in business, she hired an assistant and increased her business capacity.

JOURNAL ENTRY GUIDE #13

Use a journal to record the answers to your **business related** questions in each of the three steps above. Identify the support you need and how you will celebrate your efforts.

Excess baggage dramatically slows you down in your journey of life and work. Most likely, it is what's powerfully keeping you entrenched, until you address it.

At this point, you have realized the excess baggage you have carried in various areas of your life and business/work. With full awareness of being weighted down by excess baggage and its negative impact, you now have the necessary information to implement transformative changes.

Through it all as you implement this strategy, it is important to note the following:

Shedding of Excess Baggage is a significant decision that requires support to follow through on your actions and celebration of your efforts along the way

In summary, shedding excess baggage requires you to:

1. Choose and commit to identifying them
2. Decide to take action to shed them
3. Identify and get the support you need to follow through
4. Celebrate each step of the way.

Take Action NOW and Make It An Ongoing Habit

Take Action and Shed Your Excess Baggage
Refer to Chapter 2 to clarify and make your Compelling

Commitment Statement to motivate you towards action

Awareness of your excess baggage is important. With that awareness, taking positive action to shed it is powerfully transformative. Shedding your baggage is a two part process:

1. **Shed your existing excess baggage** – a one time series of actions to Create Space and Increase Your Positive Energy Now
2. **Consciously identify potential excess baggage as an ongoing new habit** – be aware of what can become excess baggage, choose to release old habits and avoid adding new excess baggage

Create Space and Increase Your Positive Energy Now

Make the decision to shed your excess baggage, use the journal exercise to keep track of them and secure the support you require to be held accountable for this freeing set of activities.

Make a summary list of your excess baggage in each area of your life and business/work as identified above. For each item, record:

1. The equivalent energy draining weight if you weighed the load you carry
2. The cost to continue carrying it (in time, money, energy, etc.)
3. What you will gain—or are freed up to do—once you shed it
4. Your target date for completion
5. How and when you will celebrate shedding it in your own meaningful way.
6. Use the journal guide to make your entries and use it as an action plan.

Consciously Identify Potential Excess Baggage as an Ongoing New Habit

Notice old habits of what has drained your energy from the excess baggage items you identified above. As you recognize them or any new thought that drains you of positive energy, decide to release them.

This will require practice and is worth the efforts of being conscious and intentional in developing new enriching habits.

By shedding the backlog of excess baggage and releasing new ones as you identify them, it is easier to remain focused and committed to traveling light and manifesting with ease. It will be easier to be your highest and best self and live your dream life every day.

JOURNAL ENTRY GUIDE #14

Fill in the list of activities and use it as your action plan to shed your excess baggage.

Choose to Release Old Habits and Not Add On New Excess Baggage as an Ongoing Habit.

An important note:

Shedding excess baggage is like clearing clutter in a room. You first make it a priority, schedule time to clear the existing backlog of clutter and be intentional to not create new piles.

It is easy to pile on excess baggage until it becomes a new habit to recognize and discern what is useful and what is or can become excess baggage. You will learn to easily identify excess baggage by keeping your excess baggage list in your conscious awareness; what you have shed or are in the process of shedding. Eliminating an old habit and forming a new habit requires you to consciously practice and to be patient with yourself. Goethe said:

> *"Habit is a man's sole comfort. We dislike doing without, even unpleasant things to which we have become accustomed."*

You will have many opportunities to practice your new habits. Releasing old habits requires practice and commitment to your new habits. By choosing to release all that does not serve you or your highest intentions, you will experience transformative life change. Ensure you have the loving support you need; both a sounding board and an accountability partner as you engage and sustain this significant life change.

• STRATEGY 2 •
Take Essentials With You

When you pack for a vacation, there are certain essential items you must take along for your ideal vacation time. These items are basic and absolutely necessary for your vacation to be enjoyable and to run smoothly.

For example, if your vacation trip includes sightseeing as well as other outdoor activities, essential items include appropriate and comfortable clothes for place and time of year, dress shoes as well as walking/hiking/water shoes, address book to mail postcards, travel size first aid kit, maps, travel journal, camera, sunscreen, vitamins, etc. Similarly, when you live your vacation and have the life of your dreams, you engage in activities you are naturally drawn to; activities that are done with ease and bring you deep joy. More often than not, you are your highest and best self. For this to occur naturally and authentically, it is essential to integrate your whole being, aligning your heart, mind and soul so you honor what you most value.

In your daily journey, this means having physical items, action steps, and perspective shifts readily available that reflect the:

- love in your heart
- focus of your mind
- yearning of your soul.

Let's take a closer look at the essentials that accompany you to live your vacation as part of your divine journey.

In my own divine journey, I have learned and experienced many transformations by using what I have categorized as a "First Aid Tool Kit" and 7 Core Spiritual Principles. They are transformative for my clients as well and I trust they will be transformative for you.

First Aid Tool Kit

As you go about each day, there will be times when you find it challenging to be your highest and best self. Should you need them, at your disposal is your first aid tool kit of essentials.

This First Aid Tool Kit is comprised of 3 categories of essential items:

1. Memory Box Journal
2. Inspirations
3. Wellness Aids.

Memory Box Journal

This is more powerful than you may realize.

You move through your busy life as if 'on automatic,' with little or no time for celebrations. A memory box journal is a record of the experiences that give you joy and make you smile. It can be a physical keepsake box in which you place special reminders, bringing you immediate joy when you look at the items, or a simple listing/pictures of your special joy filled memories. These joy filled memories are personal and significant to you. You can choose to access them anytime—look at them or just think about them—and you can use them over and over again.

Some people refer to this memory box journal as your emotional bank account where you can make countless deposits and withdrawals and it never diminishes. In fact, once you have this in your awareness and enjoy the experience of recording/compiling and remembering them, you will anchor the joy filled experience, inspiring you to keep making new deposits. Your memory box journal will overflow.

Why is this so important?

When we think about what gives us joy, we feel joy in that moment. When we celebrate the person/event/activity, we multiply the joy. Celebrating is a powerful way to appreciate, show gratitude and at the same time, experience joy. Feeling joy and being happy accesses a relaxed state in which you more easily remember and connect with who you are and what's really important. You gain perspective of a greater truth and your best and highest self emerges from that awakened state.

I remember at the end of one evening when our daughter Alison was feeling very stressed. She shared that she felt happy when she thought about everything she was thankful for; with that thought she fell asleep. You can imagine how thankful I was at that moment. You too can choose a happy feeling when you most need it.

JOURNAL ENTRY GUIDE #15

Reflect on everything that gives you joy and makes you smile. Write them in a special journal or in the downloadable journal guide at **www.liveyourvacation.com.** Whenever you have new joy filled experiences, return to your journal and add them to your list.

Note: Decide if a physical keepsake box will also inspire you. If so, buy make or decorate one that makes you smile just by looking at it.

Inspirations

Having sources of inspirations in your living and business/work space/environment will add joy to your day. These remind you of:

- who you are
- what's really important to you
- your connection to your highest source.

They include photos of family and friends, collages on your vision board, favorite music, wind chimes, aromatherapy diffusers, pictures of favorite places, candles, paintings, plants, special stained glass etc. You may even have a prayer corner, table or symbol that is a source of joy. Whenever you look at it, you feel joy. In those precious moments your energy shifts and you have or are open to a new perspective.

Do you already have your sources of inspiration in your home and work space? Now is the time to frame that favorite picture or comic book, compile a photo collage or any other source of inspiration you want to be in a highly visible area.

JOURNAL ENTRY GUIDE #16

Use your journal to record all your sources of inspirations and commit to follow up on any items requiring your attention.

Wellness Aids

Your health and wellness—and that of those around you—are important to living your dream life every day. I remember learning the phrase "your health is your wealth." You know the truth of how much being healthy and well means to your enjoyment of life and doing your best work. You and your business/work are connected. Being healthy requires all of you, mind, body, and spirit; all your energies flow freely and you are in alignment.

In your dream life, you have in place all that helps you assess and maintain your well being. You connect with partners on your health support team and make conscious choices. Examples of partners for your health and wellness include your doctor, dentist, naturopath, nutritionist, acupuncturist, chiropractor, fitness trainer, yoga teacher, personal and business coach, and spiritual mentor. Their recommendations may inspire you with aids for your wellness.

Intuitively, I was guided to use natural means to address my allergies and tendency toward recurring sinus infections. Aromatherapy products from Saje Natural Wellness in Vancouver have helped me, my family and countless others, and I no longer have the chronic symptoms of allergies and sinus infections. The essential oil products have become part of my wellness aids. What wellness aids are you intuitively drawn toward to integrate in your life?

Another great wellness aid is finding ways to laugh often. It's likely you have experienced how good it feels to laugh and how a tense and stressful moment can magically change with a witty comment. Laughter and a sense of humor makes you feel good, relieves stress and has a positive impact on your health and well being. Consider some of the following:

- Be around people who make you laugh
- Think of something funny
- Watch comedy shows

- Have a funny picture or mask nearby
- Join a laughter yoga class
- Regularly read or write jokes
- Develop a sense of humor by taking yourself lightly.

Use your journal to record which wellness aids you use or plan to use to maintain your good health. Commit to establishing or renewing healthy habits.

JOURNAL ENTRY GUIDE #17

I commit to the following healthy habits:

1.
2.
3.

---

7 Core Spiritual Principles

Spiritual Principles are rules or basic truths which may be intangible but when followed, positively impact you at your soul level as well as at all levels of your life and work or business. Applying these spiritual principles will be transformational for you and those around you. They support you to live your dream life every day.

To integrate some or all of them into your life requires shifts in your learned perspectives. Let me explain.

What you think about yourself, your life, your business or work determines how you feel and the actions you take as a result of those thoughts and feelings. The results of those actions are then part of your whole experience. The place where you can have an effect in the results you experience is in choosing the thoughts on which you focus. Your thoughts are part of the point of view or perspective you have. Learning to let go of one perspective and shift to another is essential to being your best and highest self so you can live your dream life every day. This learning can be from a person in your life or work, or from divine guidance.

I have two early memories of shifts in perspectives that set in motion transformational changes. These memories illustrate the early learning during my teenage years. I trust they inspire you to make your own transformational shifts.

The first memory was from my youngest sister. I came home from a volunteer activity and my dad was upset about me not being at home to help in the family business, but he had saved food for me. I did not eat but instead went to my room. I felt sad and was crying.

My perceptive and wise 5 year old sister Margaret slipped a note under the door with the message about how much Papa loved me and his gesture of saving of food that he cooked was his way of expressing his love. At that very moment, I shifted my perspective to see the truth as seen by Margaret, and that focus made a significant difference to me and my relationship with my dad.

The second memory was from divine guidance. My point of view of my much older, now deceased, father was that he must meet me half way to understand me and reach out and communicate directly to me as an all knowing dad. One day, I had a sudden thought "well, if I know more, then I am responsible for more. I am to reach out and communicate directly to him, expressing my thoughts and my love by hugging him often." From then on, I let go of the perspective that he was responsible for knowing what I was thinking and feeling and I accepted the responsibility to fully express what was in my heart. With this shift in perspective to make that decision, my life was transformed and while he was alive, I lived with no regrets about enjoying a relationship with my dad.

The following 7 core spiritual principles are shifts in perspectives; transformational for both me and my clients. Used regularly, they serve you to live your vacation every day. I am grateful to my parents, family and friends, and my coaches and mentors for all that I learned through them. Well known teachers for whom I am also grateful include Deepak Chopra, Mike Dooley, Wayne Dyer, Mark Victor Hansen, Louise Hay, Thomas Leonard, Og Mandino, Don Miguel Ruiz, Lance Secretan, Eckhart Tolle, Marianne Williamson and others. If you are not using their principles, I encourage you to consider making the shifts to implement them and experience the positive and transformational results.

1. Trust Your Intuition

> *"Follow your instincts. That's where true wisdom manifests itself."* — OPRAH WINFREY

> *"For the spiritual being, intuition is far more than a hunch. It is viewed as guidance or as God talking, and this inner insight is never taken lightly or ignored."* — WAYNE DYER

> *"The intellect has little to do on the road to discovery. There comes a leap in consciousness, call it intuition or what you will, and the solution comes to you and you don't know how or why."*
> — ALBERT EINSTEIN

Belief in a higher source, God, the universe, creator—or however you describe it—is your most powerful tool. Some describe your intuition as God speaking to you. By trusting your intuition, "gut" sense or hunch, you will not be led astray. You have this ability which can be developed the more you trust it. You may ask, how you will know if it is your intuition or something else? Your intuition has no hidden agendas and wants only what is best for you in the purest sense; it is not your mind rationalizing or your emotions revealing. Your intuition aligns with your heart, mind and soul as your divine guidance.

Upon reflection, I recognized that my intuition was always right.

Have you ever had an inkling, a sense or a momentary thought but ignored it to later find out that you had accurate information even before you realized its significance? It is well-worth the investment to pay attention to your intuition. If you are too busy to notice, it is time to slow down and become clear of distractions; externally in your physical space and internally in your noisy thoughts.

Everyone has intuitive abilities but not everyone realizes this nor has developed it by trusting and using it. As a child perhaps you did not learn to pay attention to your inklings, "gut" sense or feelings. You may have received the subliminal message just to ignore or negate your intuition. Over time, you would have forgotten about that innate ability and divine gift. If you think about the times in the past in which you ignored or compromised your intuition, you will see a distinct pattern; your intuition was 100% accurate.

With your brain producing thousands of thoughts every day and the busyness of your life, it is easy to become separated from your intuitive guidance.

The first step to rebuilding this link is to set aside quiet time; "do nothing" time. Pay attention to ask and listen to what your intuition has to say throughout your day. Once you begin to truly trust your intuition as a tool, you will use it every day, not only when you need to make major decisions. You will gain confidence over time and experience a sense of peace in trusting the wisdom of your inner guidance.

Notice what ideas come to you when you spend still time and what experiences you have trusting your intuition.

To practice this, use your journal to record and track your:

- still time experiences
- intuitive messages throughout the day
- results of acting on them.

JOURNAL ENTRY GUIDE #18

Complete the following statements:

During my still time, I thought, felt or had a vision of...

My intuitive message is calling me to...

The results of taking action on my message were...

---

2. Present is Perfect – Be Fully Present, Here and Now

Your first response may be that nothing is perfect. I too am familiar with the phrase, "No one and nothing is perfect." In fact, I used to be afraid to describe anything as "perfect."The association I made was a judgment that I was disrespecting God who is perfect and I am too flawed to be perfect. Now, I embrace the principle that the Present is Perfect.

We are each on our divine journey. This does not mean that things could not be better, or that you do not want more for yourself and others, or for your business or for your life. It does mean that you fully accept yourself and the present moment as part of your divine journey, getting ready for what's next in that journey.

This is a perfect time to address the topic of judgments.

I remember hearing God described as a fearing God who

judges, and later hearing him described as a loving God who is merciful and forgiving.

Judgments enmesh you in the past, leaving you fearful of the future; not fully alive or engaged in the present. Without judgments, you think, say, and behave lovingly to yourself and to everyone around you. You give a most precious gift that is of the highest source. When you accept the present as perfect without judgments, which are heavily loaded excess baggage, you give yourself the energy to move forward. This then allows you to be freer to receive creative ideas or wisdom to take the next step in your easy, inspired way to take action. You are also more free to receive the gifts of learning or confirmation that you are on course to living your vacation.

When you see the present moment as perfect, you have no stress. During a challenging time, your thoughts are usually of past mistakes, or future anticipation of mistakes, which lead to a present moment stress in your body. What if you see the present as perfect in the moment, acknowledge what is, feel deep appreciation for all your blessings, connect with your heart and soul's desires, and intentions, and make a choice from that place? Can you see how that moment is stress-free?

Having no stress in the moment does not necessarily mean that everything is occurring as you planned or would like. It does mean that you choose to not allow whatever is occurring to be stressful, by shifting your focus to remember to honor who you are, the people around you, and the vision of where you are headed.

Of course, depending on the situation, it may be that you get to a relaxed state and realize the gifts or blessings in disguise within a much shorter time than in the past. The principle that the present is perfect provides an inner calm, especially when you also have the faith that it is part of your evolution on your divine journey. From this place of inner calm, your best and highest self emerges. Being your highest and best self result in you experiencing joy. The more you allow yourself to feel more joy, the more you celebrate and appreciate each precious moment in the present and therefore you can live your vacation or dream life every day.

> *"Yesterday is history. Tomorrow is a mystery. And today? Today is a gift. That's why we call it the present."*
>
> —Babatunde Olatunji, a Grammy Award winning virtuoso of West African percussion

When you accept the present as perfect, you are ready to be fully present here and now. This means you are not thinking about the past, or of the future, but you are giving the present your full attention. This requires practice because we are not accustomed to giving any one activity, or one person, our undivided attention. Our lives are so full and so hectic that we multitask all the time.

While I still multitask and have a busy lifestyle, I have found that being fully engaged in the present allows me to accomplish more in less time. When I take action in my easy and inspired way, I enjoy what I am doing and I accomplish with ease.

In conversations, I have found that by being fully present and listening to others, I hear more and I allow divine guidance to flow through me. The results seem magical. You, too, can have these experiences by seeing the present as perfect and being fully present in each moment.

Just do your best.

Reflect on what you believe about the meaning of things being perfect. Decide to practice being fully present throughout your day and notice the difference it makes to you. Use your journal to record your experiences.

Please note that this takes practice. It is customary to not be fully present in the moment. Instead I propose that you decide to be aware and continually make conscious choices to not dwell on the past or to be concerned about the future. Be patient with yourself and in the moment, pay full attention and accept the moment as perfect in your divine journey, helping you prepare for the next moment.

JOURNAL ENTRY GUIDE #19

Perfect means...

Today, when I was feeling challenged, I remembered to be fully present, accepted the present as perfect and I noticed...

---

3. Express Yourself Fully and Do Not Take Things Personally

Do you remember times when you did not speak up about how you felt and what you really wanted? Do you notice how badly you feel and how unproductive, overwhelmed, and stuck you are when you take things personally?

Communicate Authenticity

Fully expressing yourself is about being authentic in every moment as you communicate who you are, in truth.

On an external level, it is more effective to be present with yourself and your business when you are being authentic. Consider the following:

Does what you wear fully express your authentic self?

Do your business related materials fully express the core of your business?

From your business perspective, does your business fully express and align with who you are, what you stand for and the difference you make for others?

On an internal level, you are fully expressing yourself when what you think, say, or do align with what's most important to you and your core values. When you are clear about your core values and are conscious about choosing to express them, your communications will be authentic.

If you are not already clear about your core values, now is the time to become clear so you can be conscious about fully expressing yourself. Use the following list of values my clients have shared to help you identify your core values. You may have other ones as well.

Adventure	Freedom	Loyalty
Beauty	Friendships	Love
Compassion	Fun	Making a Difference
Contributing	Generosity	Optimistic Outlook
Creative Difference	Harmony with the Environment	Peace
Creativity	Health	Prosperity
Diligence	Honesty	Quality
Excitement	Humor	Service
Exploring	Integrity	Spiritual Connection
Faith	Justice	Timeliness
Family	Leadership	Teaching
Financial Serenity	Learning	Truth
Fitness	Kindness	Understanding

JOURNAL ENTRY GUIDE #20

My core values are...

My actions align with my core values of...

I easily orient my life and work in new ways around my core values of...

Effective Communications

Your communications are effective when what you intend to communicate is understood as you had intended. (You may also have unexpected positive results.) For many different reasons this is not always easy. Each person's experiences, frames of reference, and perspectives are different and there may be factors that may or may not be related to how messages are received or understood. Sometimes, you may find it difficult to fully express what you think and later wish you had done so sooner. Understanding behaviors—your own behavioral style as well as those of others—helps you become more clear about yourself, allowing you to adapt your behaviors to enhance your communication.

Self awareness is the first step toward communicating effectively. With this insight, you will know what is effective and ineffective and can share that with others to improve your relationships.

There are assessment tools available to help you move from making inaccurate assumptions and taking things personally to communicating more effectively and improving your relationships. You can also work on this on your own.

Make two lists:

1. How you *like* people to communicate with you (examples include: get to the bottom line and do not give me long stories unless I ask, be direct, respectful and factual, illustrate with credible references, etc.)
2. How you *dislike* people to communicate with you (examples include: do not be condescending, do not just stick to the facts, do not be unorganized in your presentation, do not ramble or you will lose me etc.).

If you prefer a detailed customized assessment, inquire at **www.peaksuccesscoaching.com** for options available to you or your team.

JOURNAL ENTRY GUIDE #21

- Identify those with whom you want to improve your communications.
- Record your list of Effective Communications and Ineffective Communications.
- Decide if you want to use an assessment tool and identify your options to do so.

Listening Is a Creative Force In Communication

Up to this point you may not have been fully expressing yourself for a variety of reasons. These include but are not limited to:

- your perception of what's expected in your family, your
- religious or work cultures

- your concern about what others may think about you or your fears about their reactions
- unawareness of your core values or your behavioral style
- misreading another's words or actions.

Actively listening is a key skill in having heart-centered conversations. Expressing yourself fully and not taking things personally require that you are fully present to the other, listening for the deepest truth, sharing your curiosities and asking for clarity.

> *"Listening is a magnetic and strange thing, a creative force. When we really listen to people there is an alternating current, and this recharges us so that we never get tired of each other. We are constantly being re-created."* — BRENDA UELAND

Taking things personally gets in the way of listening for the truth. Often you over react and don't respond in a way that honors everyone. What you take as personal is really something else unexpressed, inaccurately expressed, or a trigger from a past memory unrelated to the person in front of you. What if you choose to hear everything as just information to help you in some way? What if none of what is being said is ever about you? Your best self will be present and your conversations will be enjoyable and honoring. With practice, this authentic way of having conversations will become more automatic for you.

Here is a distinction that will help you be more effective in your communications; the distinction between *reacting* and *responding*.

When you take things personally and react, you do not inspire the brilliance in you nor do you see the brilliance in the other person or the valuable information that can inspire you. So the next time you are ABOUT to REACT, stop, take a deep breath and ask yourself: What is the gift for me in this and how would my highest and best self RESPOND? This happens in seconds or minutes and will get easier with practice. Your communication will be much more effective. Try it and experience positive results!

4. Everything Happens For The Highest Gifts of All

> *"I trust that everything happens for a reason, even when we're not wise enough to see it."* — Oprah Winfrey

You may question this and find that embracing it requires practice. However, by choosing this perspective, your attention is focused on looking for the opportunities or gifts of the situation, instead of the distraction of what is neither useful nor helpful.

This perspective reminds you that you are on your own divine journey and everything that happens is part of that journey. This means that:

- You connect with who you really are and with your purest intentions
- You take action from that pure place
- You surrender to a higher power.

Yes, I know at the moment of whatever happened you are not likely to immediately say it happened for the highest gifts of all. That's okay, you are human and that reaction is normal. Here are some helpful points to remember:

- Whatever you feel at the time is neither right nor wrong
- Acknowledge the feelings you have and give yourself permission to feel whatever you are feeling
- If you have learned the habit of keeping it all in, it is important to release this from your body to gain clarity and perspective
- Write about how you feel and what you are thinking, even if you shred it afterwards. If painting or drawing about it helps, then

do that. It's a simple way to release it and to gain clarity.

- A trusted friend, mentor, priest, pastor, rabbi, or coach is able to help you to gain perspective and see the gifts of whatever has occurred. Check with your inner guidance to reveal the identity of this person.

5. Every Challenge is an Opportunity Bearing Gifts of Inspiration

> *"Opportunities to find deeper powers within ourselves come when life seems most challenging."* — Joseph Campbell

Often, a challenge or problem results in stress until you find a solution or the problem goes away. However, from a conscious perspective, when you view a challenge or problem as an opportunity bearing gifts of inspiration, this gives you direct access to your creativity by looking for an outcome that improves you, your business and your relationships.

Then, you powerfully choose where to focus your mind's attention and authentically make heart- and soul-centered decisions. Consequently, stress is minimized and your conscious choices lead to rewarding results, which are often pleasantly surprising.

The following two verses are from a prayer song I find empowering. It reminds me of my choices to experience inspiration:

"We are called to act with justice
We are called to love tenderly,
We are called to serve one another;
To walk humbly with God!

Come! Open your heart!
Show your mercy to all those in fear!
We are called to be hope for the hopeless

So all hatred and blindness will be no more"
— WE ARE CALLED, page 95 in St. Helen's Church, Burnaby, BC Canada Hymnal

Here are three helpful tips to more quickly find gifts of inspiration:

i) Do not spend time waiting for the answer to "Why?" if it does not reveal itself quickly.

The "Why" question is helpful when you learn something from the experience. However, when the answer is not apparent quickly, spending more time asking only prolongs your stress and distances you from the gifts.

ii) Switch your attention from 'What is not' to 'What is' and focus on what you have to be thankful for. Celebrate!

Wherever your mind is focused is where you see manifestation. So when you focus on the challenge as a problem and all that is not working (I have done that as well but now happily much less so), you are moving in a direction that causes you stress.

With practice, in the moment of any challenge, it has become automatic for me to now always ask the question, *"What is the gift/opportunity/lesson for me now?"*

Sometimes, the answer comes instantly or later that day or after I speak with my coach; I always see the gift or have an inspiration and you can too. When my clients focus on what *is* working, who they *are,* what they *have done*, and what they *do have*, they find there is more to celebrate than they originally realized. They free themselves to be inspired by the challenges and see the "blessings in disguise."

I encourage you to ask the same question as you face any challenge and enjoy the results.

iii) Maintain a sense of humor

Laughing at yourself or the situation shifts your energy from getting stuck and feeling no joy to attracting creative solutions—or lessons—and feeling much joy. I encourage you to laugh more or call someone who helps you laugh more.

You will have many opportunities to practice this. I heard that it takes 21 consecutive days for a new habit to be formed. Write in your journal each challenge you face and practice asking the question *"What is the gift/opportunity/lesson for me now?"* for the next 21 days. Record the corresponding gift(s) you recognize.

JOURNAL ENTRY GUIDE #22

Spend a few minutes to think about a challenge you are currently facing. Ask yourself the question: "What is the gift/opportunity/ lesson for me now?" Experience the gifts of inspiration to record in your journal.

---

6. Be of Service to One Another – Your Easy and Inspired Way

> *"Your talent is God's gift to you. What you do with it is your gift back to God."* — LEO BUSCAGLIA

This quotation on the wall of Mrs. Jozsa's kindergarten class caught my eye. The message stayed with me long after our daughter Alison was in her class.

Serving others with my talents has brought me unlimited joy. We are each meant to discover our talents and our unique ways of expressing them as we serve others. When you do this you automatically create wins for all. It is also a way of *being* during every interaction you have with others.

It is important to note that being of service to one another means serving **your self** as well as serving others. Let me explain more about this very important point.

When you fully know and act upon this, it will be as transformative for you as it has been for me and my clients.

You are born a masterpiece! You are worthy! You and your life matter! Take a few moments right now and let those thoughts permeate your whole being.

Knowing and living your passion and purpose means you are to serve yourself with your talents, as well as being of service to others. When you serve yourself, you lovingly nurture your heart, mind, and soul. As a result, you have radiant joy. Taking action to serve others from that unshakeable, powerful, and inspired place will not only give you joy but also adds to the collective good and enhances lives.

Serving yourself may feel like a selfish thing to you. Selfish as a learned label of judgment usually means a self-centeredness that assumes one does not care about others and possibly harms others. With that meaning, it is reasonable to feel guilty or not want to be selfish. That definition then translates to ignoring, depriving, and depleting yourself, of thinking of others first and repeatedly saying yes to others and no to yourself. However, the truth is that by taking extremely great care of yourself, physically, emotionally, intellectually, and spiritually, you have the best to give when you serve others.

You may be skilled at caring for others first and caring for yourself last and must now unlearn it, as I did. Taking extremely great care of yourself is not a bad, selfish thing but a most honoring and inspiring practice that supports you to be at your best and ready to be of service. (Note that whatever you choose to do to be of service to yourself and others is to be done in your easy and inspired way.)

What does taking extreme care of you look like? Perhaps it's committing to:

- be still in your favorite place and do nothing for 30 minutes daily
- pamper yourself with regular aromatherapy baths and visits to the hair salon, spa, sauna, hot tub or whatever pampering means to you
- enjoy a hobby or learn a new skill, e.g. reading, hiking, golfing, biking, swimming, fishing, boating, learning a foreign language, etc.
- sign up for regular fun, exercise, yoga, Pilates, cardio kickboxing, kayaking, playing bridge, golfing, skiing, swimming, etc.
- meet with friends regularly
- spend quiet time in nature to meditate or pray
- make regular appointments with your doctor, dentist, acupuncturist, chiropractor, massage therapist, or other wellness professional.

At first you may resist doing this with thoughts of already having so much to do. You might also think some of it is a frivolous use of your time and money.

As Johann Wolfgang von Goethe said,

> *"Whatever you can do or dream you can, begin it. Boldness has genius, power and magic in it. Begin it now"*

Begin with the easiest step for you. You are worth it; your family, friends and the world deserves to have you at your best!

Several years ago I was doing too much and not consciously integrating all aspects of my life. Even the thought of slowing down for 10 minutes to do nothing was very difficult for me. However, I committed to it and it was the beginning of a transformation for me.

You and the ripple effects of your impact on the world deserve this gift of your extreme self care. Make a list of what this means for you and the results you would experience. Use the journal entry exercise to record and celebrate this as a toolbox you return to often and identify how you best serve others.

JOURNAL ENTRY GUIDE #23

Extreme self care means...

When I make the commitment, I will experience...

I am committing to...

I will celebrate each of my commitments with...

At my best, I will serve others by...

When you are in the habit of taking great care of yourself, it is easier to see more clearly the truth in any given situation, to be patient and to shine your light to be of service to others.

As a conscious entrepreneur, you know your business reflects a marriage of your skills, talents and service to others to make a positive difference in the world. Everyone wins doing business with you. When designed around your strengths, you choose your inspired and easy way of doing anything. Naturally you will accomplish more with much less effort.

The world awaits you serving fully in your effortless and inspired way.

7. Ask for Help – Your Ideal Support Team

Being your highest and best self, and doing the best work you are destined to do, requires a foundation of support from a multitude of sources. You are never alone. You must have your best support team of heaven and earth combined. *Of heaven* is a regular connection to God, your most powerful source. *Of earth* are those whose Godlike spirits are a best fit for you and what you are to accomplish in your most effortless and inspired way.

Asking for help requires the clarity of knowing what you want, having the faith that others want to help, courage to ask and confidence in your ability to be of service in the highest way in which everyone wins.

To help you begin to identify your ideal support team, customize the following list:

Your biggest and highest source of help — God, or however you identify that powerful source ______________________________

Family members ______________________________

Friends ______________________________

Business or work partners ______________________________

Colleagues ______________________________

Home maintenance ______________________________

Household chores ______________________________

School age children care ______________________________

Mentor ______________________________

Coach ______________________________

Identify your ideal support team members and record them in your journal.

Spend some reflection and planning time to identify those tasks with which you need help and who can potentially help you. At this point you may notice a warning flag if the thought of asking for help immediately triggers any of the following conversations in your head:

- I can do it myself
- I should be able to figure it out myself
- I don't want to look or be thought of as not capable
- If I ask for help, I may be turned down and I will be embarrassed
- It will cost me too much money; how will I pay for it?

You will accomplish more with more ease when you focus your time on doing what you are best at doing; ask for help from others with what they are best at doing. Everyone wins. The benefit of asking for help will be personal to you.

The following are some examples to get you started on identifying those tasks for which you are willing to ask for help. These examples include: handling of administrative tasks, technical support needs, doing routine household chores, committing to a healthy lifestyle and giving up smoking, calling a buddy to celebrate the clearing of clutter in your personal and work environments, team building tools, coaching support for valued employees, personal shopping, understanding the children, men and women in your life, car pooling, etc.

An important success tip when you ask for help is to ask with clarity and be unattached to the outcome or results. As Deepak Chopra states:

> *"Anything you want can be acquired through detachment, because detachment is based on the unquestioning belief in the power of your true Self."*

JOURNAL ENTRY GUIDE #24

Complete the above list of your ideal support team members. You may add other categories now or later as needs are identified.

Record what you will ask for help with and take appropriate actions.

CHAPTER 4

Staying Awake for the Journey

Secret Revealed

DOES "VACATION" TO YOU MEAN GETTING AWAY from home to be relaxed? Are you happy and excited about and during the time away?

After discovering who you are, shedding your excess baggage and deciding what to take on your vacation, you are ready to take the journey.

Dorothy, in the classic story *The Wizard of Oz,* wanted to go home and discovered that inside herself was what she needed all along. The Lion, the Tin man, and the Scarecrow also went in search of what was already inside themselves.

You too have what you need to live your vacation every day without having to leave home physically. That's the secret!

You don't have to leave home to live your vacation every day. You design your life and your business/work in such a way that allows you to take actions to be your best self, shine brilliantly in the most natural ways, and to be HAPPY.

Decide to BE HAPPY and start taking action NOW. Experience the transformations in this commitment to yourself. Decide to be your best each day, do the best you can to make the best of each day, LOVE and APPRECIATE yourself and everyone in your life, and experience joy every day.

As Mike Dooley states in *Infinite Possibilities:*

> *"The secret to living the life of your dreams is to START living the life of your dreams."*

Start now and enjoy the journey!

Staying Awake for the Journey

On your divine journey, you've likely discovered that when you are living your vision and doing work you love, you feel joy, time passes easily, and there is a natural feel to what you do. Nothing feels like "work." Chances are you can recall how much of a journey it was to simply arrive at the decision to commit to your business and life vision. Until you do that, your journey is a completely different one.

Before committing to remaining awake on your journey, you may have seen opportunities as obstacles, or compromised your intuition to make a quick decision you hoped would move you forward. Many of my clients express feeling alone with their thoughts prior to working with me. You may feel the same way if you don't have the right support systems around you.

When you're awake on your journey, you evolve differently than those around you. Other people, who don't understand your journey, may express their fears about your decisions and not support you in your life or entrepreneurial pursuits. Yet, you cannot be pulled off track. You possess an inner wisdom, a deep knowing that you are destined to pursue your life and your business. Somewhere along your journey, you became open to learning and raised your awareness of how empowering it was to shift your perspectives and experience dramatically different results. These are the gifts of staying awake on your journey.

Staying awake is about making conscious choices and empowering yourself. When you make conscious choices to shift your perspective, your life will be transformed.

How the Principles Work - Read the Directional Signs and Be Ready to Change Course

"Even when you think you have your life all mapped out, things happen that shape your destiny in ways you might never have imagined" — DEEPAK CHOPRA

When you are awake, you are ready to recognize when a change of direction is needed or you get confirmation you are right on track with your plans. Sometimes, things do not go as planned and you find yourself pushing too hard. You may feel that you are "spinning your wheels" and going nowhere. When you get a variety of signs, this is a clear indicator that it is time to slow down or change course.

You will recognize some of these signs when you:

- lose your keys and are frantic looking for them when you are late
- twist your ankle or fall going down steps or stairs you have taken hundreds of times before
- encounter traffic everywhere you go
- feel devoid of energy
- get more customer complaints than usual.

Handling your stress and transforming your fears are where you get to apply the practical guiding principles to live your vacation every day. Your stresses and fears are directional signs loaded with information to give you direction and move you forward in your life and business journey.

Handling Stress *(Memory jogger)*

"Tension is who you think you should be. Relaxation is who you are" — CHINESE PROVERB

Being stressed is when you forget who you are and you are disconnected from your divine source of power.

Many clients have shared that they are usually positive and have faith. When stressed however they become negative, fearful and think of the worse possible outcome. It is possible to be free of stress during and following a problematic situation. While this may be easier said than done, it does take practice and it is possible to be relaxed and not feel stressed in the midst of what was once very stressful.

Here is an example of how applying the essential principles worked for me. See how it might support you as well.

Awhile ago, I was scheduled to lead a workshop at a staff retreat. Usually I take a printed copy of the driving directions with me when I drive to a new place. For whatever reason, perhaps because I remembered it to be only a 5 minute walk away from the ferry dock, I did not take them. When I drove off the ferry and after driving a few minutes into town, I did not see any signs for the lodge. Even though I had enough time to keep looking, I decided, following my intuition, to stop and call for help with directions. It was then I learned that notification of over booking at the lodge had fallen through the cracks and that I needed to return to Burnaby where the retreat had been relocated. I had to quickly get back on the same ferry.

It would be perfectly normal to react and lay blame, get stressed and have worried thoughts of being stuck on the island, late for the workshop or missing it all together, and having to reschedule, which for 26 people would have been difficult, etc.

What happened instead was that I made it to the same ferry going back, arrived at the workshop early, calm and ready to carry on. Everyone felt badly and apologized.

Upon reflecting about what I had chosen to do naturally; taking deep breaths, being thankful for making the call to ask for help, getting back on the same ferry, and maintaining my vision of doing the workshop as the focus of my attention. I reminded myself that everything happens for the highest gifts of all and every challenge is an opportunity bearing gifts of inspiration. By the start of the workshop, I realized the gifts and inspirations.

I experienced living my vacation of being calm and unstressed, the power of forgiveness and not laying blame and shame. The experience ended up as a teaching moment to include in this book and in the workshop: the synchronicities of divine help in getting me back to Burnaby safe, early, calm and energized to carry on was well received by the participants.

The 3 step **TLC** *process for you to use anytime you feel stressed*

Take deep breaths to re-center yourself and feel relaxed, remembering who you are and accepting the moment

Look with your mind's eye to connect with your vision/goal/ what's important

Count your blessings and be thankful at that moment for something and look for the gift/opportunity as this is part of your divine journey.

A few examples of memory joggers that will serve as quick reminders of who you are and to do the 3 step process are:

1. Pay attention to your body signals such as any discomfort or tightness
2. Have something meaningful with you to touch such as a stone, a ring, a rosary bead
3. Think of a word/phrase/image that is symbolic of who you are at your highest and best self calm, relaxed, excited, and at peace such as pure love, brilliant star, compassionate, powerful beyond measure, or being at a beach/mountain or lake which is your peaceful and happy place.

In your business, how you handle stress impacts the way you do business, including your staff and customers. One area which can be especially stressful is receiving negative feedback from staff or customers. Whether in your personal or business life, when taken personally, feedback feels like criticism. Shifting your perspective is an effective approach to welcome and invite feedback. You can choose to view feedback as information to inspire your evolution or your business's growth.

Good Health As An Absence of Illnesses/Diseases

Have you noticed that you get sick after experiencing a stressful period in your life? This is because stress depletes your body's immune system. Your immune system protects you and keeps you healthy. When under stress, your body is fighting to keep you alive and suppresses your immune system.

Prolonged periods of stress result in illness. Therefore, it is important to immediately and effectively manage stress when it occurs.

After you handle any stressful situation, be sure to cancel out any associated negative memory by creating a positive memory and add it to your Memory Box Journal (Chapter 3).Being in good health is a necessary part of living your vacation and the life of your dreams every day.

Therefore, it is critical to your good health and wellbeing to identify what stresses you, the changes you can and will make, the help you need, the cost of doing nothing and the benefits of using a system to manage your stress. Excessive baggage causes you stress and shedding that (as in chapter 3) eliminates the source of stress.

Here is a transformative way of being to stay healthy:

When we remember who we are and our connection with

our source and one another, we are open to be healed. A powerful reminder for me came in the form of a healing message from Fr. Vincent Cutrara of St. Helen's Church in Burnaby, BC Canada:

> *"We are resolved to the oneness with God and with other people for which we were made...."*

I love the meaning of the word "Namaste." It serves as a memory jogger that we are one with each one and with God.

Starlene, Reiki Master/teacher shares,

> *"Namaste comes from the Sanskrit word namahte. Namaste is pronounced Nam-a-stay. In Sanskrit namah means "bow, obeisance, reverential salutation, adoration."*

One of the translations I heard some time ago that also resonates with me: *The spirit in me greets the spirit in you, a place where we are one.*

Use the journal guide exercise to record and become clear of your stresses and your commitment to take action.

JOURNAL ENTRY GUIDE #25

Complete the following:

I feel stress when...

When this occurs, I will...

Transforming Fears *(Truth seeker)*

Although it is normal to have fears, our fears often prevent us from feeling joy. They paralyze us.

When you are fearful, you are stressed, you do not see the truth and you are not in the energy of love, of being your highest and best self. Essentially, you are not living your vacation.

Howard Thurman, author, philosopher, theologian, educator and civil rights leader said,

> *"Don't ask what the world needs. Ask what makes you come alive, and go do it. Because what the world needs are people who have come alive."*

Sometimes doing what makes you come alive is filled with fear of failure, overwhelm, judgment and much more. It is even possible that you have forgotten what it feels like to be fully engaged and alive every day. If you are not already doing what makes you come alive each day, now is the time to begin.

What makes you come alive? How are you honoring your highest purpose?

You may have heard or read of the acronym for F.E.A.R. (False Expectation/Evidence Appearing Real).Think about that. Do you recall the many times you invested your precious energy being stressed about what you anticipate will happen or what you experienced in the past, projecting that into the future, only to find out that it never materialized? You are not alone in doing this.

When Fear is present, love or loving energy, is absent. What that looks like is included but not limited to the following examples:

- Not making that marketing call…fear of personal rejection
- Not saying how you feel or not sharing an idea…fear of being ridiculed or criticized

- Not applying for a new position…fear of failing or losing something you have
- Not feeling as confident or competent as you really are…fear of being compared with others
- Not making a change…fear of losing your reputation or losing yourself
- Not addressing a priority…fear of the unknown success or failure
- Not taking time for fun…fear of losing control or not feeling you deserve to take the time
- Not taking the risk to reveal your humanness or a mistake you made…fear of losing love forever or of not being accepted.

Remember, while fears seem very real, they are illusions that serve a purpose.

Eleanor Roosevelt said,

> *"We gain strength, and courage, and confidence by each experience in which we really stop to look fear in the face."*

Raise your consciousness, acknowledge the fear as a fear and face it by looking for the truth. This may be outside your comfort zone. In fact it may be so scary that you feel stuck, overwhelmed or paralyzed. You do not have to be alone; ask for the help you need to be in the energy of love so you more confidently take the action(s) to move you forward. Fear keeps you stuck and clouds your vision. Courage is required to address fears and acknowledge the truth. Speaking the truth means you are vulnerable. My clients have experienced the powerful results that transformed their lives when they took positive action to communicate the truth to those who mean the most to them.

It is worth the risk—you and your loved ones deserve to be

happy now, not later. Will you take the risk?

Identify your fears and keep track of the situations when they appear, rate their intensity, identify the greater truth, and identify the related decisions/actions. Celebrate the person you are.

JOURNAL ENTRY GUIDE #26

Record and track your fears and transformations in the journal table provided in the guide.

The following quote serves as a purposeful reminder of the powerful impact we have in freeing ourselves to be our best and highest selves while inspiring others.

> *"Our deepest fear is not that we are inadequate. Our deepest fear is that we are powerful beyond measure. It is our light, not our darkness that most frightens us… There is nothing enlightened about shrinking so that other people won't feel insecure around you. We are all meant to shine, as children do… And as we let our own light shine, we unconsciously give other people permission to do the same. As we are liberated from our own fear, our presence automatically liberates others."*
>
> — MARIANNE WILLIAMSON

The truth of what Marianne Williamson shared is very powerful. You will experience transformations by acting on the insight and stepping into your brilliance, the Masterpiece you were born as, with your gifts waiting to be authentically and uniquely expressed.

Be prepared that your fears will surface just before you are about to step into something bigger than you have experienced before; your brilliance.

Sometimes, you may even experience a big roadblock as if you are being asked if you are ready to truly honor your commitment to your dreams.

Take a deep breath and remember that you are meant to be true to yourself and others, show up powerfully and share your gifts with the world.

This requires a decision to be happy, to be in the energy of love in your most effortless of ways, to seek the truth and to shine brilliantly. What if all of your actions were guided by that decision? When you get feedback from others or hear your own inner voice, rejoice and ask deeper and deeper questions to seek the truth.

By applying the 7 core spiritual principles, you too have the choice of transforming your fears and living your vacation every day.

CHAPTER 5

Celebrate Every Day

THE EBBS AND FLOW OF LIFE, THE YIN AND YANG of everything is natural; every moment will not be blissful. So even with knowing who you are, shedding your excess baggage and taking along the essentials to live your dream life every day, there will be challenges.

A key element to ensure your success to be your best and highest self every day is to celebrate each day and be HAPPY. When challenged, and things do not go smoothly or as positively as you want, and you begin to feel like you are moving backwards, know that you are not going backwards. You are doing your best and you are on your divine journey, so decide to be happy in the moment and take action from that decision.

Thriving Environment and Daily Habits

A plant blooms naturally when all conditions in its environment are present. You also will thrive with ease when your daily habits honor what you most need. Your daily habits provide the environment for you to thrive. When aligned with your core values (as identified in chapter 3) these habits give you joy and you will more easily see what there is to celebrate. This may include:

- A wakeup routine saying what you are grateful for and feeling deep gratitude
- Meditation or prayer to connect with the highest source of your power and to visualize your dream life for which you are grateful

- Healthy eating habits
- Physical activity that is fun for you
- Quality time with your family
- Enough sleep
- An end of day routine recognizing and appreciating the gifts of that day.

Identify the elements of your thriving environment and the daily habits that will give you joy and feed your spirit. Within each, note what action you will take for it to become a new habit. Decide to make this a priority and use the journal to record your commitment. Remember to ask for help from your support team to help you to be accountable. Celebrate your joy and successful new habits.

JOURNAL ENTRY GUIDE #27

The following daily habits give me joy…

My accountability partner is…

Count Your Blessings

When you look for blessings, you will see blessings. Appreciate. Appreciate. Appreciate. Appreciate everyone in your day and you will see more blessings and feel more joy.

I know there are times when others may say or do something that you do not appreciate. You can choose to not react but to respectfully respond by expressing yourself fully and not take things personally. At times, you may choose to just listen and say nothing. Instead, you will shift your perspective and ask yourself, "What will make me happy in this moment and is it for the good of all concerned?" When you choose to be happy, you will see more blessings to celebrate, even if the celebration is being happy with yourself for choosing to take the high road and transform a negative to a positive experience.

Reenergize-Rejuvenate

Pay attention to your energy throughout the day. When you need to reenergize yourself, have readily available what will give you joy and a boost of energy, similar to the function of an energy bar you eat. This is a reserved list of what will bring a smile to your face or reading or remembering the contents of your Memory Box Journal.

Make a list of anything and everything that makes you smile and choose from that list when needed. It may include the thought of your child or of your pet, children carefree and building sandcastles on the beach, family members getting along harmoniously, sharing fun times with friends, a kind word or gesture from someone, something yummy, like chocolate covered strawberries, thinking of the positive difference of your work, a beautiful sunrise or sunset, your favorite song or a piece of music, a walk in the rain, the view from a mountain top at the end of a hike, a hug you received etc.

Note: Refer to and update your ***Journal Entry #15*** *(Chapter 3).*

Celebrating every day is about enjoying the journey of your life and work, having fun, feeling deep gratitude for who you are, what you have and everyone in your day, being happy and loving in your thoughts, words and actions.

CHAPTER 6

There is No Place Like Home

WHETHER IT IS GOING HOME, BEING AT HOME OR enjoying home, is this the home feeling you have or yearn for?

You feel joy, safe, relaxed, loved, free to be you. You are "*comfortable in your own skin*". You feel whole, fully heard and free to express your deepest fears and greatest joys. You love unconditionally and feel loved unconditionally. You are surrounded by people you love, you are in an environment you love, and doing what you love when you want. That "at home" feeling all boils down to one of being happy, knowing your worth, and being in the energy of love. You are part of a whole, giving and receiving in loving ways. You have heard the phrase "*Home is where your heart is*" and your heart is full of love. The heart accurately symbolizes love. Nothing but love exists in your heart and when it is open, you and those around you feel its loving energy. Discover this love within you and every day will be filled with joy. You then love yourself, your life, your business, those in your life and your connection to a higher source of love.

As you know, sometimes we forget who we are and get caught up or stuck in the challenges of the moment. When you are not accepting the moment, not celebrating and loving what is in your present moment, you are unhappy and not in the energy of love; you are disconnected from one or all the sources of love. You will not feel love when your heart is closed.

Going home is your journey inward, loving and being proud of who you are.

Being at home and enjoying home is about being happy and loving NOW, not later. Later is when the grass is greener on the other side and you postpone your happiness until then.

What feels like home to me is when I am being unconditionally loving and kind and I have an extra smile when others are unconditionally loving and kind to me and to each other. The feeling is of being at peace with myself and all is well in my world. The satisfaction I feel wherever I show up and say YES, I am fully present and engaged with the purest of energy and I allow my communication and action to flow through me. I know that from my highest and best self, I help elevate everyone else. This happens when I am fully conscious and connected to who I am, trusting God's guidance, free of excess baggage and consciously integrate the spiritual principles in this book. Some days this is 100% of the time and 90-95% on average.

Can you see the world I see? From our heart and soul, we will see the same loving world. Join me in faith and trust.

There is indeed no place like home. Decide and choose right now what shift in perspective you need to make or what action you need to take to live each day from feeling at home with your highest and best self, the Masterpiece you are. Then experience the magical transformation of living your dream life every day. You and the world deserve for you to be your highest and best self, to be fully YOU everyday.

Let's review the 6-step approach to make every day a vacation day:

1. Experience the journey within and discover who you are and your relationship with others
2. Define your destination and clearly see the vision of your life and work
3. Shed your excess baggage to complete the past and take along the essentials tools for today
4. Remain awake on your journey, read the directional signs and make corrections as necessary

5. Celebrate every day
6. Realize that there really is no place like home; choose to be happy and loving now

Living your dream life every day is a journey every day.

This book is meant to be read several times. You may choose to read all the steps again, go to a specific step or just open the book and read whatever page you open.

Each time you read it, you will discover or be reminded of something important for you in that moment.

Enjoy your journey!

CLOSING INSPIRATIONS

I WANT TO SHARE A FEW CHINESE PROVERBS THAT reflect the essence of living your dream life every day.

May you and all your loved ones enjoy good health, happiness and prosperity!

When the heart is at ease, the body is healthy.

If you want happiness for an hour—take a nap.
If you want happiness for a day— go fishing.
If you want happiness for a month—get married.
If you want happiness for a year—inherit a fortune.
If you want happiness for a lifetime—help someone else.

If you want 1 year of prosperity, grow grain.
If you want 10 years of prosperity, grow trees.
If you want 100 years of prosperity, grow people.

INVITATION FROM GLORIA

Establish Your Instant Vacation Group!

Purchase 7 Live Your Vacation Books and get 7 FREE to share with your family, colleagues and friends.

JOURNEYING TOGETHER IS MORE FUN AS YOU HAPPILY relate to others. You are energized by your social interactions. Your dream life feels complete.

This offer is only available to those who go to the website to order. Purchase 7 copies. Receive 7 extra copies FREE! Go to **www.liveyourvacation.com/free**

The reason I extend this offer relates to my destiny. My destiny is to help create a more peaceful and loving world by empowering and inspiring others to see the masterpiece they are and to be their best and highest selves. Therefore I want you and as many people as possible to awaken to the masterpiece you/they are and to live your soul's purpose using this Live Your Vacation book as one of your guides.

Also for each book sold, a portion of the proceeds is donated to The Rotary Foundation of Rotary International to help fund Rotary Peace Fellowships. Join me in creating a more peaceful and loving world.

Your help in spreading the word means a lot to me and I appreciate you in advance. May you and your loved ones experience good health, happiness, joy and prosperity in abundance!

FREE RESOURCES

Secrets to Inner Peace, Harmony & Joy

If you have enjoyed much success, but still experience a deep yearning for inner peace and peace in all your relationships, this special report is for you. It is part of a FREE success package at **www.PeakSuccessCoaching.com**

Enter your name and email address at the top right hand corner of the website.

Peak Success Inspirations

Do you enjoy reading inspirational quotations via email? Peak Success Inspirations is Gloria's FREE gift delivered every two weeks as timely reminders of what you already know at a deep level to support you being your best and highest self. It is part of a FREE success package at **www.PeakSuccessCoaching.com**

Enter your name and email address at the top right hand corner of the website.

---

7 Strategies Conscious Entrepreneurs Need To Know To Be Productive &Effective Without Sacrificing Time with Themselves, Family or Friends

Did you follow your entrepreneurial spirit to launch your own business because you love the freedom and creativity it provides? However, you find yourself working too many hours and yearn for more personal time or time with family and friends? Most entrepreneurs would love to have it all, and can! Download this special report and see that the success you want is possible.

Enter your name and email address at the top right hand corner of the website **www.peaksuccesscoaching.com**

CONTACT

GLORIA TOM WING STAUDT

Phone:	604-523-6268
Email:	info@peaksuccesscoaching.com
Online:	www.twitter.com/PeakSuccess
Main Website:	www.peaksuccesscoaching.com
Other Websites:	www.liveyourvacation.com www.operafromthesoul.com

For quantity discounts, promotions or sponsorship of *Live Your Vacation*, please call 604-523-6268

ABOUT GLORIA

GLORIA TOM WING STAUDT IS AN INSPIRATIONAL success coach and an enthusiastic leader of an award winning Burnaby Metrotown Rotary Club. As an entrepreneur, she makes a significant difference by using practical applications of spiritual wisdom for measurable results. Through her business, she provides coaching, facilitation, strategic direction and assessment services via telephone, internet and in person.

At an early age Gloria intuitively realized that her destiny is to help create and empower others to create a more peaceful and loving world. She does this through her commitment to live her highest purpose and to be of service to the world, with God as her center. Mahatma Ghandi's words *"Be the change you want to see in the world"* inspire her daily. She lives with her family in British Columbia, Canada.

Facing the ups and downs on her journey to inner peace, harmony and joy, she feels blessed and finds it easy to be loving and generous. And now, she dedicates her life and work to passionately guiding others on their spiritual journeys. Her gifts lead them to the ease and joy of being at home with themselves as they live their highest purpose, becoming loving and generous as a result.

Her products and services include seminars, books, retreat workshops, breakthrough coaching conversations, Strategic direction consultation, coaching programs, speaking, writing and editing. She is a contributing author of *Conscious Entrepreneurs – A Radical Approach to Purpose, Passion & Profit.*

QUICK ORDER FORM

Online: **www.liveyourvacation.com**

Fax: **604-523-6267**

Phone: **604-523-6268**

Please send ______ copies of *Live Your Vacation* (US $17.95, CDN $19.95)

Name: ____________________

Address: ____________________

City: ____________________

State/Province: ____________________

Zip/Postal Code: ____________________

Country: ____________________

Telephone: ____________________

Email Address: ____________________

TAXES

Canadian Residents, please add 12% HST tax for products shipped to Canada (GST/HST # RT0001 - 862844123)

SHIPPING & PROCESSING (S&P)

Shipping will be determined by destination; S&P will be added

PAYMENT

☐ PayPal ☐ Credit Card

PayPal Account/ Credit Card #: ____________________

Name: ____________________

Expiration Date: ____________________

3 or 4 digit CID number on card: ____________________

Signature: ____________________